CULTURES OF THE WORLD
Honduras

Leta McGaffey and Michael Spilling

Marshall Cavendish
Benchmark
New York

PICTURE CREDITS

Cover: © Keren Su/ Danita Delimont Stock Photography
alt.type/Reuters: 30, 34, 36, 41, 94, 101, 119, 120, 121 • Bes Stock: 8, 27, 45, 47, 52, 86, 93 • Bjorn Klingwall: 38 • Chip & Rosa Maria de la Cueva Peterso: 33 • Corbis Inc.: 10, 12, 14, 15, 20, 26, 28, 32, 39, 42, 57, 67, 68, 71, 80, 89, 116, • Getty Images: 11, 37, 44, 46, 49, 50, 51, 53, 59, 74, 76, 90, 113, 118, • Lonely Planet Images: 5, 56 • National Geographic Images: 24, 111 • Photolibrary: 1, 3, 6, 7, 9, 13, 16, 17, 18, 19, 22, 23, 25, 48, 54, 55, 58, 60, 61, 62, 63, 66, 69, 70, 72, 73, 77, 78, 79, 82, 84, 87, 88, 91, 92, 95, 96, 98, 99, 102, 103, 104, 110, 112, 114, 115, 122, 124, 126, 128, 129, 130, 131

PRECEDING PAGE

A wooden bridge brings people atop the beautiful waters of the Bay Islands.

Publisher (U.S.): Michelle Bisson
Editors: Deborah Grahame, Mindy Pang
Copyreader: Sherry Chiger
Designers: Nancy Sabato, Lynn Chin
Cover picture researcher: Connie Gardner
Picture researcher: Thomas Khoo

Marshall Cavendish Benchmark
99 White Plains Road
Tarrytown, NY 10591
Website: www.marshallcavendish.us

© Times Media Private Limited 1999
© Marshall Cavendish International (Asia) Private Limited 2010
® "Cultures of the World" is a registered trademark of Times Publishing Limited.

Originated and designed by Times Media Private Limited
An imprint of Marshall Cavendish International (Asia) Private Limited
A member of Times Publishing Limited

Marshall Cavendish is a trademark of Times Publishing Limited.

Library of Congress Cataloging-in-Publication Data
McGaffey, Leta.
  Honduras / by Leta McGaffey and Michael Spilling. — 2nd ed.
      p. cm. — (Cultures of the world)
  Includes bibliographical references and index.
  Summary: "Provides comprehensive information on the geography, history,
    wildlife, governmental structure, economy, cultural diversity, peoples,
    religion, and culture of Honduras"—Provided by publisher.
  ISBN 978-0-7614-4848-8
  1. Honduras—Juvenile literature. I. Spilling, Michael. II. Title.
  F1503.2.M34 2010
  972.83—dc22   2009022642

Printed in China
7 6 5 4 3 2 1

CONTENTS

INTRODUCTION

THE TROPICAL COUNTRY OF Honduras is a place of spectacular biodiversity, with unspoiled beaches, magnificent mountains, and many plant and animal species living in its lush rain forest. It is also home to the Copan ruins, one of the greatest Mayan archaeological sites in Central America. The people of this beautiful country are vibrant and diverse, tracing their ancestry to Amerindian, African, and Spanish backgrounds. The history of Honduras, however, is one of hardship and poverty, with long years of colonial exploitation followed by decades of underdevelopment and lack of investment. Despite the growth of a thriving manufacturing sector in recent years, Honduras is still essentially a rural country dominated by the rigors and poverty of agricultural life. Despite its misfortunes, the country has a peaceful political climate that few of its more volatile neighbors have been able to match, and Hondurans are a warm and gracious people who are always ready to welcome visitors.

GEOGRAPHY

The dreamy blue waters of the Caribbean Sea along the northern coast of Honduras.

THE REPUBLIC OF HONDURAS is a beautiful, mountainous country approximately the size of the state of Ohio or Pennsylvania, with an area of 43,278 square miles (112,090 square kilometers). It is the second-largest country in Central America, bordering Guatemala in the west, El Salvador in the southwest, Nicaragua in the southeast, and the Caribbean Sea in the north, with an extensive coastline of 510 miles (820 km).

Although the Caribbean lowlands make up only 15 percent of the land, they support 25 percent of the population of Honduras.

One of the numerous bay islands of Honduras.

Hills and mountains in various shades of green in a valley outside Copán.

There is also a small gulf in the southwest off the Pacific Ocean—the Gulf of Fonseca—with a coastline of 95 miles (153 km). Honduras stretches between 13 and 16 degrees north of the equator and between 83 and 89 degrees west longitude. Honduras is a country of natural diversity with rugged mountains, vast pine forests, idyllic beaches, flat savannahs (treeless grassland), coral reefs, and acres of fertile banana fields.

TOPOGRAPHY AND GEOGRAPHICAL REGIONS

There are four distinct geographical regions on mainland Honduras as well as the unique Bay Islands off the north coast. Over two-thirds of Honduras consists of interior highlands with dramatic mountains and valleys. The Mosquito Coast, near the Nicaraguan border, is covered with dense rain forest. Along the Caribbean coast, there is a stretch of long, narrow lowlands where thousands of acres of banana plantations thrive. Just off the Gulf of Fonseca in the south there is a smaller area of lowlands as well.

INTERIOR HIGHLANDS The most prominent feature of Honduran topography is the interior highlands, made up of extinct volcanoes. Mountainous terrain makes up over 80 percent of the land. This is where most of the population lives, although the mountains are difficult to travel through and to cultivate.

A major mountain range called the Cordillera Merendón runs from the southwest to the northeast. The highest peaks are found here, including the highest mountain, Cerro Las Minas (also called Pico Celaque), which is 9,350 feet (2,850 meters) above sea level. The Cordillera Nombre de Dios range lies south of the Caribbean shore. It is not as rugged as the Merendón range but has peaks rising to 7,988 feet (2,435 m) above sea level. The Cordillera Entre Ríos is another mountain range. It forms part of the border with Nicaragua.

Scattered throughout the interior highlands are numerous flat-floored valleys, 1,000 to 3,000 feet (300 to 900 m) above sea level. These fertile valleys support farming and livestock rearing. Subsistence farming has been relegated to the slopes of the valleys, while the large farming businesses work the more arable, broad valley floors in an effort to increase the country's exports.

It is common to see cattle grazing in the lush pastures of Honduras.

A coastal village lies alongside a mangrove forest in the Gulf of Fonseca.

Villages and towns, including the capital city of Tegucigalpa, have been built in the larger valleys. The Sula Valley is an extensive depression that runs from the Caribbean to the Pacific, providing a relatively convenient transportation route.

PACIFIC LOWLANDS The smallest geographical region of Honduras, the Pacific lowlands, is a strip of land only 16 miles (25 km) wide on the north shore of the Gulf of Fonseca. This fertile plain was formed from volcanic soil washing down from the mountains. Cattle ranches make use of the savannahs. Mangroves along the shore provide breeding grounds for shrimp and shellfish. Two islands in the Gulf of Fonseca—El Tigre and Zacate Grande—have volcanic cones that rise to over 2,296 feet (700 m) above sea level.

CARIBBEAN LOWLANDS Hondurans refer to the Caribbean lowlands as "the north coast," or simply "the coast." This region has been by far the most exploited area, but development accelerated in the late 1800s when the banana industry flourished.

The central part of the lowlands is narrow, only a few miles wide. To the east and west of this area, however, is a wide coastal plain where banana plantations abound. The alluvial plains and coastal sierras produce rich crops of fruits and vegetables.

LA TIGRA NATIONAL PARK

As the first national park of the country, La Tigra National Park is a popular destination for day trippers from Tegucigalpa. It is a cloud forest preserve for a large variety of plant and animal life. The park's moss-covered world of trees laden with bromeliads, orchids, and ferns lends a feeling of mystery. The many mammals include tapirs, monkeys, and the rarely seen ocelot and jaguar. The park is also home to many colorful birds, including the resplendent quetzal, the emerald toucan, and the cinnamon-bellied flower-piercer. Visitors to La Tigra can hike miles of well-maintained, well-marked trails past a scenic waterfall and an abandoned silver mine or traverse the length of the park via a lookout point with an impressive view of Tegucigalpa.

MOSQUITO COAST This vast area of Honduras is one of Central America's last frontiers of untamed wilderness. Indigenous people, including the Garifuna, Pech, and Miskito Indians, still inhabit this hot, humid region on the eastern Caribbean coast, which blends into mountain slopes. It is difficult to reach by road, and the most common forms of transportation are by airplane or boat. The dense rain forests of this region have been exploited to the danger point by logging. The Caratasca Lagoon—a large body of salt water connected to the Caribbean by a narrow inlet—is located here.

THE BAY ISLANDS Together, these islands make the perfect tropical island paradise. They are lush emerald islands crowded with palm trees and surrounded by the turquoise Caribbean Sea. There are three large islands—Roatán, Utila, and Guanaja—three smaller islands—Helene, Morat, and Barbareta—as well as a biological reserve on the island of Cayos Cochinos. There are also more than 60 islets scattered in the area.

An aerial view of Utila Island.

The Bay Islands are the tips of ancient underwater volcanoes. These islands have a diverse geography, ranging from mountains covered in dense jungle to outstanding barrier reefs that attract divers and snorkelers from all over the world. The rainy season on the islands lasts from October to as late as February. March and August are the hottest months, but during the rest of the year, gentle sea breezes cool the air. Some of the islands are uninhabited, some have a few people living on them, and some are being developed for tourism.

Roatán is the largest, most populated, and most developed of the Bay Islands. It has a long, irregular mountain range inland with peaks that reach 770 feet (235 m). There are also hillside pastures, limestone caves, and clumps of lush green forest. White sandy beaches and cliffs make up the north shore, while sandy inlets and bays punctuate the south shore. A beautiful, protected barrier reef that circles the island draws many tourists. The people live along the coast, many in white clapboard, tin-roofed houses on stilts. There are a few culturally rich villages. These are located near historical sites that tell interesting tales of the first pirates to invade the Bay Islands. The economic hub of Roatán is French Harbor, a town that is home to the largest fishing fleet in this area of the Caribbean.

The vivid underwater world of the barrier reef off Roatán Island draws divers from around the world.

The flooded Río Ulúa delta after Hurricane Mitch.

RIVERS

Rivers mark half of Honduras's borders with El Salvador and Nicaragua. Numerous rivers drain the highlands during heavy rainfall and have carved out wide, fertile valleys, but there is only one natural lake—Lake Yojoa. The most important river is Río Ulúa, which is 249 miles (400 km) in length and flows northeast through the Sula Valley into the Gulf of Honduras. In some areas, such as the Biosfera del Río Plátano, river travel is the main way to penetrate the region.

CLIMATE

The interior highlands have tropical wet and dry seasons. Almost all the rain falls during the wet season from May to September. Tegucigalpa, located in the highlands, has a pleasant climate ranging from 86°F (30°C) in April, the warmest month, to 73°F (23°C) in January, the coolest month. As elevation increases, temperature decreases. Above 6,562 feet (2,000 m) there is sometimes even frost after a cold night.

HURRICANE MITCH

In October 1998 a terrible natural disaster hit Honduras as Hurricane Mitch rampaged across the country. The rare Class Five hurricane, with winds of up to 180 miles per hour (290 km per hour), began its destruction of Honduras when it sat for two days over Guanaja, one of the Bay Islands, which was devastated. By the time it reached the mainland, it was classified as a tropical storm. However, the amount of rain that was dumped onto almost every inch of Honduras (up to 4 feet [1 m] in many areas) created mudslides that literally buried whole villages, highways, and roads, and wiped out most bridges in the country. The cap of an extinct volcano fell off due to the rains and wiped out the villages in its path. Honduran cities and villages were left totally isolated except by air.

The storm killed an estimated 6,600 people in Honduras. A week after the storm had subsided, 11,998 people were still missing and 1.4 million were left homeless and living in crowded shelters on high land. The hurricane wreaked havoc on the fertile Aguan and Sula valleys, destroying thousands of acres of banana and palm plantations. Approximately 70 percent of the nation's crops were destroyed—some fruit companies on the Caribbean coast lost 100 percent of their crops. Over 60 percent of the nation's infrastructure, including major bridges, was demolished. The total damage to infrastructure alone, not including loss in exports, was estimated at $2 billion.

Amid the devastation, Hondurans counted their blessings. Roatán, one of the most developed areas of Honduras and a major tourist draw, was left relatively unscathed. The El Cajón Reservoir regained its optimal level, allowing the country's thermal generators to work at full capacity without imported oil. Aid poured in from countries around the world to Honduras and other Central American countries that were badly damaged by the hurricane. Many countries wrote off debts owed to them by Honduras and its neighbors in an effort to help them rebuild their homelands.

Bromeliads cover the branches of trees in a cloud forest in Honduras.

The Pacific lowlands also have wet and dry seasons, with year-round high temperatures between 82°F (28°C) and 90°F (32°C). The dry season occurs between November and April, usually the hottest months of the year. During the rainy season the high humidity makes the heat uncomfortable.

The Caribbean lowlands have a tropical wet climate with high temperatures and humidity and rainfall year-round. These conditions have made the Caribbean lowlands ideal for growing bananas and pineapples, which need warm, wet weather. The only relief from the hot weather comes in December or January, when there are high winds but only slightly cooler temperatures. The Caribbean coast is particularly prone to hurricanes and tropical storms, because Honduras lies within the hurricane belt (an area of the Atlantic Ocean prone to hurricanes). These storms usually travel inland from the Caribbean. Hurricanes occasionally form over the Pacific, but these are usually less severe, if they come over land at all.

FLORA

Honduras, like any tropical country, has a variety of vegetation that amazes people from temperate climates. Honduras's forests have only recently been set aside as national parks and biological reserves. On top of mountains and along ridges are cloud forests. These "weeping woods," as they are called, catch the moisture in the air, creating an ideal environment for ferns, vines, orchids, and broadleaf plants to grow. A rich layer of decaying matter covers the forest floor, and bromeliads (a type of flowering plant) flourish in the crooks of trees. Many varieties of wild avocado grow in abundance in varying moisture conditions.

Near these humid peaks are patches of desert that are deprived of moisture because the cloud forests catch all the water. At lower elevations pines and firs cover the mountain sides. In the savannahs of the northeast are acacias and cacti, while in the warmer and wetter lowlands are mahogany, Spanish cedar, rosewood, palm trees, and mangroves. Besides avocadoes, tropical fruit that grow in abundance include tamarinds, mangoes, pineapples, guavas, papayas, and of course, bananas.

FAUNA

Honduras's great variety in climate allows for a wide variety of mammals, fish, birds, amphibians, reptiles, and insects to live in the country.

Honduras has many of the forest animals that are found in the United States, but it also has some exotic mammals. These include brocket deer, raccoons, coyotes, armadillos, foxes, squirrels, porcupines, monkeys, jaguars, and other large cats. There are also animals found only in tropical America, such as the kinkajou, a tree-dwelling mammal with brown fur and a prehensile tail, also called the honey bear.

It takes an early riser to spot the elusive quetzal. Just after dawn these resplendent birds drop out of the trees in the cloud forest to eat a breakfast of blackberries.

A kinkajou sitting on a branch.

The national bird of Honduras, *la gacamaya*, or the scarlet macaw.

Honduras is home to a wide variety of snakes, including the boa, worm, coral, bushmaster, rattlesnake, and fer-de-lance. There are also many species of brightly colored frogs and toads. Crocodiles, caymans, manatees, and salamanders live in and near the water. Many turtles, such as the huge leatherback, live either in the sea or on the shore. Lizards are found everywhere. Little hand-sized geckos make their home anywhere, and iguanas can grow up to 6 feet (1.8 m) long.

Lake Yojoa has large black bass that provide excellent game fishing. Sharks, catfish, barracudas, grouper, and mackerel are just a few examples of the ocean life found in the Caribbean Sea and the Gulf of Fonseca. There are mollusks such as snails, lobsters, and freshwater crabs.

More than 700 species of birds are found in Honduras. Of note are swallows, the green ibis, the tiger heron, spotted wood-quails, cuckoos, macaws, quetzals, and a beautiful cloud forest trogon with iridescent red and green feathers and long tail feathers that arc like a peacock's.

There are many species of butterflies, moths, beetles, spiders, bees, wasps, ants, flies, and mosquitoes, many of them brightly colored.

CITIES AND TOWNS

Honduras is the only Latin American country that has most of its urban population distributed between two large centers: Tegucigalpa and San Pedro Sula. Although Honduras is still primarily an agrarian society, these two cities have grown considerably since the 1920s as Hondurans have migrated from rural areas to find jobs. The cities contrast dramatically: Tegucigalpa is the political capital, whereas San Pedro Sula is the industrial and commercial center. Other cities in Honduras include La Ceiba, Copán, Santa Rosa de Copán, El Progreso, and the largest port, Puerto Cortés.

There are numerous towns in the western half of Honduras. Many of them are set amid splendid countryside and have interesting historical and native legends. Small towns such as La Esperanza, Gracias, and Santa Lucía attract a steady stream of tourists.

TEGUCIGALPA The capital city of Honduras, Tegucigalpa, is built into the hills of the central highlands. It became the capital city in 1880.

Tegucigalpa has the flavor of a small colonial city, with brightly colored houses built into the hillsides and narrow, winding streets. At the center of the city are Spanish colonial churches; many government buildings, including the National Palace and the Presidential Palace; and numerous schools. This landmark historic center includes the Plaza Morazán, often called Parque Central, with a statue of the national hero Francisco Morazán. Overlooking Tegucigalpa is the United Nations National Park on Picacho Mountain. This park is recognized for its magnificent gardens of tropical plants and flowers, including beautiful Honduran orchids. Residents of Tegucigalpa flock to the park on Sundays, and use the outdoor grills for picnics.

Tegucigalpa experienced near-crippling population growth beginning in the 1950s when the population increased by 75 percent. More than 1.3 million people live in Tegucigalpa's sprawling metropolitan area. Many of them today still have inadequate housing and either do not have running water or receive an inadequate supply.

For all practical purposes Tegucigalpa is the capital of Honduras. However, Chapter 1, Article 8 of the Honduran Constitution states, "The cities of Tegucigalpa and Comayagüela, jointly, constitute the Capital of the Republic."

Tegucigalpa got its name from two Indian words, *teguz* ("hill") and *galpa* ("silver"), because it was originally a small mining town.

Rows of banana crops in San Pedro Sula.

SAN PEDRO SULA, the industrial capital of Honduras, is the bustling center of business transactions. It is located in the flat, fertile Sula Valley surrounded by banana plantations, and it has almost half a million residents, with as many as 1,187,000 people in the metropolitan area. The population of this city is more multicultural than the rest of the country. The San Pedranos, as they call themselves, are friendly, outgoing, and helpful to foreign visitors.

San Pedro Sula was founded in June 1536 as an agricultural town. Its importance increased quickly with the growth of fruit companies on the north coast, and the city has become the center of agricultural business for the region. San Pedro Sula is perhaps the fastest-growing city in Central America.

The city has modern glass towers as well as residential areas where stately homes with green lawns offer an old-world charm and people stroll along tree-lined avenues in the evenings.

PUERTO CORTÉS The largest and most important port in Honduras, is also the most modern port in Central America, with large container facilities that stretch for 16 miles (26 km) along the bay. It is only a two-day sail from New Orleans or Miami. Puerto Cortés grew quickly in order to accommodate the export of bananas, and later as a center for oil refining. It also has numerous manufacturing companies that export products such as baseballs and luxury sailing boats.

LA CEIBA   Nestled on the narrow coastal plain between the Cordillera Nombre de Dios and the Caribbean coast, La Ceiba is surrounded by banana and pineapple plantations. Many people go there to visit as a starting point to get to the Bay Islands. La Ceiba got its name from a large ceiba or silk-cotton tree that used to stand on the coast before the development of the docks. Traders used to congregate there to buy and sell in the shade of the big tree. It also has an international airport.

COLONIAL TOWNS   Many towns in Honduras were established during the Spanish colonial period. A few grew to the extent that they are now important for government, industrial, or commercial reasons. Other towns are better known as colonial heritage sites.

Comayagüela, about 52 road miles (84 km) northwest of Tegucigalpa, was the second capital of Honduras. It is famous for having numerous churches, including the Iglesia la Merced, the first church built in the country during the 16th century.

Considered the center of western Honduras, Santa Rosa de Copán is surrounded by mountains and national parks. It is a small, cool, very Spanish mountain town with El Calvario, a 200-year-old church; cobblestone streets; and tile-roofed houses. It was once famous for its tobacco farms, but today it is better known for its coffee.

Suyapa, just outside the capital, is called the religious capital of Honduras. A legend here tells of the miraculous discovery by a peasant of a tiny clay statue of the Virgin of Suyapa, the patron saint of Honduras.

Trujillo, located close to where Christopher Columbus first landed on mainland America, was the first capital of Honduras. Spaniards fought off pirates from a Spanish fort there. The ruins of this fort overlook the bay.

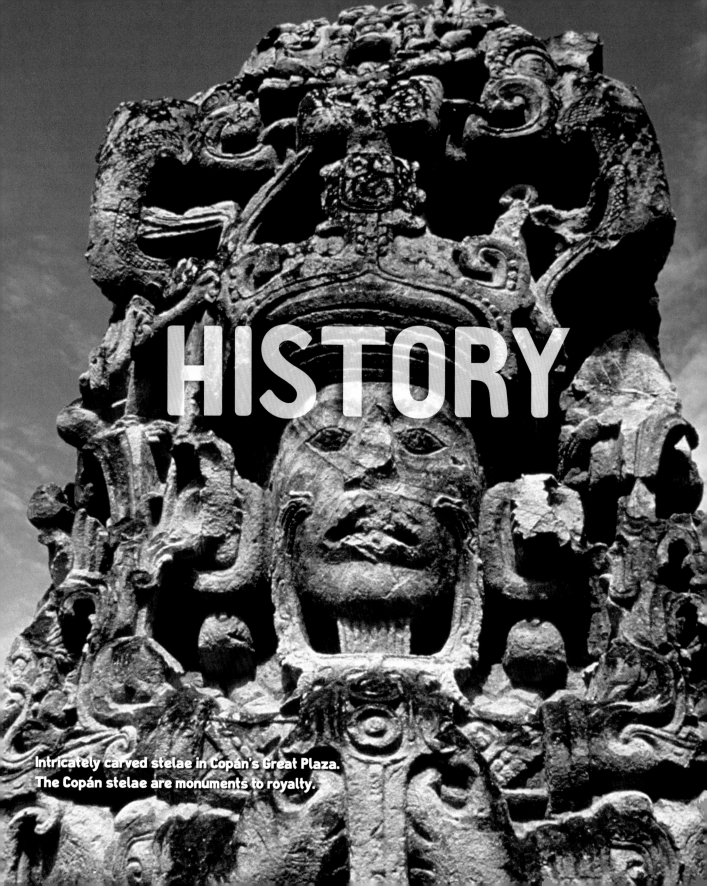

HISTORY

Intricately carved stelae in Copán's Great Plaza.
The Copán stelae are monuments to royalty.

MUCH OF HONDURAN HISTORY has been taken up with the struggle to bring together diverse peoples and cultures with assorted languages to create a unified nation. The mountainous geography made it difficult for groups who settled in different areas to communicate, and therefore it took a long time for cultures to form similarities that would eventually evolve into a Honduran identity.

The Mayan ball court at the ancient city of Xukpi in Copán is the second-largest in Central America. One of the most remarkable features of the ball court is a hieroglyphic stairway illustrating the history of the Copán royal house.

Honduras has also been extremely poor for most of its modern history. Despite these challenges, Honduras has had a more peaceful history than most of its Central American neighbors.

PRE-COLUMBIAN SOCIETY

Because Central America is a midway point between North and South America, people of various cultures have passed through Honduras over the centuries. Many of them eventually settled down in this region. Before Europeans reached Honduras, the land was populated by groups of people who spoke unrelated languages and whose customs were different.

Over 10,000 years ago people first arrived from possibly Asia or Polynesia. These settlers were probably hunters who lived in caves and simple dwellings. Thousands of years later agriculture was introduced. The first crop was most likely corn, which is still a staple today.

The most advanced and notable early inhabitants were related to the Maya of the Yucatán and Guatemala. The Mayan civilization reached Honduras in the fifth century A.D. and spread rapidly through the Río

These beautifully carved Mayan statues guarded the tomb of a royal scribe.

The Spanish fort of San Fernando de Omoa in Honduras.

Motagua Valley in western Honduras. The Maya established extensive networks of trade throughout the region, spanning as far as central Mexico. The money of the Maya was probably the cacao bean, still a local product. The ancient western Honduran city of Copán became a center for Mayan astronomical studies, mathematics, and art. One of the longest hieroglyphic inscriptions was found at Copán.

Copán was apparently abandoned at the height of Mayan civilization. Many Maya stayed in the region, but the high priests and rulers suddenly vanished. From this point on, Honduras was dominated by one indigenous group after another. These groups were often hostile toward each other. Because the different indigenous groups were always fighting for power, there was no distinct center of authority at the time of conquest by the Spanish. By subduing and allying themselves with different groups, the Spanish were able to take over the region.

SPANISH CONQUEST

First contact with the Spanish occurred during the final voyage of Christopher Columbus's expedition in 1502. Columbus sailed past the Bay Islands, and it is believed he made contact with indigenous nobility there. He then sailed on to the mainland coast of Central America and set foot in Punta Caxinas on August 14, 1502. He named the place "Honduras," a loose translation of "deep waters," which was a reference to the depth of the bay off the north coast. There was little European exploration of Honduras for the next two decades.

Interest in Honduras only began as a result of rivalries among Spanish military leaders in Central America, who were too far away for the emperor in Spain to govern. An expedition headed south from Panama, and in 1523, Gil Gonzáles de Avila discovered and named the Gulf of Fonseca in honor of the Spanish bishop Juan Rodríguez de Fonseca. Expeditions organized by Hernán Cortés (c. 1485—1547) also came from Mexico. One of these expeditions, led by Cristóbal de Olid, first conquered Honduran territory and established a settlement there on May 3, 1524.

Rival Spanish expeditions invaded Honduras and fought to become supreme, not only over the indigenous people, but among themselves. Hernán Cortés left Mexico in 1524 to deal with the conflict in Honduras and establish his authority. He temporarily restored some order by getting a few indigenous chiefs to submit to his authority and then he began to set up Spanish towns. As soon as he left nearly two years later, the strife resumed.

Hernán Cortés (c. 1485-1547) was one of the first Spaniards to attempt to govern Honduras.

COLONIAL PERIOD

By the early 1530s the indigenous people of Honduras were being killed off by disease, mistreatment, and shipment to the Caribbean Islands as slaves.

The discovery of gold and silver in Honduras in 1536 attracted new settlers who demanded local labor for their mines. This forced labor led to a major uprising by the indigenous people led by Lempira, a young chieftain of the Lenca tribe. His courage inspired many other native groups to revolt, and the battle raged for two years. Lempira was eventually murdered by the Spanish. Today he is a national hero. The monetary unit of Honduras was later named after him.

Indigenous resistance died down after Lempira's revolt failed. The revolt had also resulted in the deaths of even more of the native population. In 1539 an estimated 15,000 indigenous people were under Spanish control, but two years later there were only approximately 8,000 still alive.

The Spanish settlement of Honduras expanded in the 1540s as the fighting among rival Spaniards decreased, and the first bishop of Honduras was named. Comayagüela was made the capital of Honduras on December 20, 1557, replacing Trujillo. The key economic activity was mining for gold and silver, but some cattle ranching began as well. The indigenous people who were brought to work in the mines came from different villages all over the region. Because the indigenous population was so small and the Spanish wanted a larger labor force, African slaves were brought in. Everyone was forced to communicate in the language of the masters—Spanish. The old ways were mixed with the new Spanish ways and a new culture was born.

However, gold and silver finds became scarce and mining began to decline in the 1560s. Honduras became a province of the Captaincy General of Guatemala and remained so until it won independence from Spain in 1821.

Old colonial buildings such as this one in Garcias can be found in Honduras. Garcias is a town settled in 1536 by the brother of Spanish conquistador Pedro de Alvarado.

Francisco Morazán (1792—1842) served as president of the United Provinces of Central America for two terms and was its last president as well. He is considered the father of Central America for his major role in defending the original union of the five states that now make up Central America. Streets, parks, and cities are named after him throughout the region.

Morazán was born in Tegucigalpa. He received little formal schooling but educated himself well enough to practice law and get a position in the state government of Honduras, where his political career began.

In 1827 he led his Liberal Party against the army of the Conservative Party, defeating it in 1829. The following year he was elected president of the United Provinces of Central America. He started radical programs to improve education and the justice system, and attempted to promote economic development for the region. His plans for reform included reducing the influence of the Roman Catholic Church in state affairs.

Morazán struggled to strengthen the federation, but disputes increased, and his dream of a united, harmonious alliance ended in 1838. He was executed on September 15, 1842, after an attempt to restore the federation.

The discovery of silver in the 1570s briefly revived the economy, and Tegucigalpa began to rival Comayagüela in size and importance. Mining efforts were hampered by the limited size of gold and silver deposits, a lack of capital and labor, the rugged terrain, and bureaucratic regulations

José Trinidad Cabañas (1805—71) is considered a hero for his attempts to reunite the Central American federal government. He was president of Honduras for two separate terms—March 1 to July 6, 1852, and December 31, 1853, to June 6, 1855. Cabañas was born a creole (mixed race), the son of José María Cabañas and Juana María Faillos. He was a Liberal politician whose role in Honduran history began during the civil war of 1826—29, when he was second-in-command to Francisco Morazán.

His second term as president was noteworthy for the very first attempt to build a railroad in Central America. He was supported by the common Honduran people, but his liberal beliefs and their support were not acceptable to the Conservatives who then held power in Guatemala. Interference in Guatemalan affairs led to his overthrow by the Guatemalans in 1855.

Cabañas fled to El Salvador, where he remained politically active. He was responsible for a political uprising in El Salvador as late as 1865.

and incompetence. By the 17th century Honduras was being neglected and became a poor Spanish colony. A major problem for the Spanish was the English pirates along the Caribbean coast during the 17th century. Eventually the English began to settle on the Bay Islands and along the coast. Spain regained control of the Caribbean coast, but the English settlers remained.

INDEPENDENCE

The early years of independence were characterized by political instability. The long-standing rivalry between Tegucigalpa and Comayagüela kept the people of Honduras divided. Spain granted Honduras independence, along with the other Central American provinces, on September 15, 1821. Honduras and the other Central American countries briefly became a part of the Mexican empire, but broke away from Mexican rule after a coup in 1823 and established the Federal Republic of Central America, with the capital in Guatemala City. The first president, Manuel José Arce (1786—1847), was elected in 1825. Francisco Morazán, a Honduran military hero, was elected president of the federation in 1830. In 1834 he moved the capital to San Salvador.

José Cecilio del Valle is considered a hero in Honduras. He wrote the declaration of Central America's independence from Spain in 1821.

Honduran men carrying bunches of bananas from a plantation.

The 1830s saw constant conflict between the Liberal and Conservative parties of the region. After a Conservative revolt led by Rafael Carrera (1814–65) in 1838, the federation was dissolved. Honduras declared independence on November 15, 1838. By January 1839 it had adopted a constitution, although there was little sense of nationhood. All attempts to restore the federation after this 1838 split failed.

For Honduras the period of federation had been a time of local rivalries, ideological disputes, political chaos, and the disruption of its already fragile economy. This instability attracted ambitious politicians from within and outside Central America. For most of the rest of the 19th century El Salvador, Guatemala, and Nicaragua interfered in Honduras's internal affairs. Six constitutions were implemented and presidents were imposed and deposed by Nicaragua and Guatemala. The frequent changes of government made Honduras unstable.

BANANAS

At the end of the 1800s banana traders in New Orleans looked to Honduras as a reliable supplier of commercially grown bananas and founded the Standard Fruit Company. In the north, along the Caribbean coast, banana plantations began operation. Honduras soon became the world's leading exporter of bananas. The banana companies became more important than the government for many Hondurans because of their domination of commercial life in the area and worker welfare system. Bananas remained the mainstay of the modern economy for many years.

THE GREAT BANANA STRIKE

In 1954 Honduran workers at a Caribbean port asked for overtime wages for loading bananas onto a boat on a Sunday. Their request was refused, but they loaded the boat anyway. The following Sunday a similar incident occurred. Officials noticed a slowdown in work but foolishly ignored it. As the unrest grew President Juan Manuel Gálvez became concerned and sent soldiers to the Caribbean coast. This action angered the workers, and within a week one of the banana companies had lost all its workers. The strike spread to other banana companies, a tobacco plant, a mining company, and several clothing factories, all American-owned. The strikers held out for three months. When officials finally made concessions, work resumed with shorter hours, overtime pay, medical benefits, and paid vacations. Workers in Honduras had learned that they were a powerful political force.

In Tegucigalpa, power remained unstable and revolts repeatedly broke out against the government. Nicaragua became more and more involved in Honduras in the early 20th century. When its army invaded the country in February 1907, the U.S. government intervened to protect the North American banana trade. President William Howard Taft sent U.S. Marines to Puerto Cortés in 1911.

In the 1923 election for a new Honduran president no candidate won a majority of the votes, leaving the country on the brink of civil war. The United States stepped in again, and a new election was held in which the newly formed conservative National Party took power. In 1932 General Tiburcio Carías Andino (1876—1969) became president in a peaceful, fair election and remained in power until 1949, ruling with an authoritarian hand. Early in the Carías regime, Panama disease dramatically damaged the banana industry, while the Great Depression and World War II cut off the banana trade and the fruit rotted on the docks.

In 1954 banana workers went on strike following a labor dispute, causing a severe strain on the nation's economy. Initial government efforts to end the strike failed and work stoppages spread to other industries. The strike ended when workers were granted better benefits and the right to bargain. After decades of domination, the strike decreased the power of the fruit companies.

MODERN HONDURAS

In 1957 yet another constitution was enacted and Ramón Villeda Morales (1909—71) of the Liberal Party became president. Under Villeda many schools were built and labor rights were strengthened. A social security system was installed, but it provided medical care and pensions for only a limited number of workers. In December 1960 the Central American Common Market was formed to aid trade between the countries of the region, and restrictions on imports were lifted. Many products that used to be imported were now regionally made. However, after years where the only development was around the coastal areas by the fruit companies, Honduras lacked a wider road network, a railroad system, and a proper banking system, and most factories were established in Guatemala, El Salvador, and Costa Rica—Honduras was left behind.

On October 3, 1963, a military coup put air force colonel Oswaldo López Arellano in power. Congress was dissolved, the constitution was suspended, and planned elections were canceled. The United States promptly broke off diplomatic relations with Honduras. In 1978 a new junta (military committee) headed by General Policarpo Paz García seized the government, promising to return Honduras to civilian rule. In April 1980 military rule began to wind down; a constituent assembly was convened and an election was planned.

THE SOCCER WAR

Border disputes have long been a problem in Central America. Honduras has rarely been the aggressor, but in 1969 a border dispute with El Salvador erupted into a brief war. The Honduran government believed that Salvadorans had taken advantage of the open border with Honduras and had gained property under the agrarian reforms that were taking place in Honduras. This land was only supposed to go to people who were Honduran by birth.

The dispute is called the Soccer War because, at the time, Honduras and El Salvador were engaged in a three-game elimination match for the World Cup preliminaries. Fights broke out at the games, and both countries were insulted and enraged. Honduras decided to suspend trade with El Salvador. The territorial dispute was finally resolved by the International Court of Justice (ICJ) in 1992, which awarded most of the disputed territory to Honduras. In 1998, the two countries signed a treaty to confirm the borders agreed by the ICJ, and in 2006 the demarcation was completed.

Demonstrators march through the streets of San Pedro Sula in 2008 during a protest against violence and crime in Honduras.

Meanwhile violent revolutions were occurring in neighboring Nicaragua and El Salvador. The United States supplied weapons to Honduras in response to the left-wing Sandinista victory in Nicaragua, and the U.S. military staged maneuvers in Honduras to scare off any potential Nicaraguan incursions. After the conflict the decrease in U.S. military spending in Honduras left the country in an economic crisis once again. Rafael Leonardo Callejas Romero (b. 1943) of the National Party scored a clear victory in the 1989 election, and he began to deal with the economic situation. The rising cost of living contributed to his party's defeat in the 1993 election. Carlos Roberto Reina Idiaquez of the Liberal Party, who became president, continued the work begun by Callejas. He was succeeded in January 1998 by Carlos Roberto Flores Facusse, also of the Liberal Party.

Just when the political climate appeared to have settled, calamity struck in the form of Hurricane Mitch in November 1998. The storm left Honduras in dire straits, with the country's crucial farming industry severely damaged and the country's infrastructure weakened.

In recent years crime and gang violence have become serious problems in Honduras. In 2002 Ricardo Maduro Joest was elected president. He introduced tough policies to fight increasing crime and corruption. In 2006 Manuel Zelaya was elected president on an anti-crime, anti-gang platform.

LEADERS OF HONDURAS SINCE 1933

Tiburcio Carías Andino	1933—49
Juan Manuel Gálvez Durón	1949—54
Juan Lozano Díaz	1954—56
Roque Jacinto Rodríguez Herrera	1956—57
Ramón Villeda Morales	1957—63
Oswaldo López Arellano	1963—65, 1965—71
Ramón Ernesto Cruz Uclés	1971—72
Oswaldo López Arellano	1972—75
Juan Alberto Melgar Castro	1975—78
Policarpo Paz García	1978—80, 1980—82
Roberto Suazo Córdova	1982—86
José Azcona Hoyo	1986—90
Rafael Leonardo Callejas Romero	1990—94
Carlos Roberto Reina Idiáquez	1994—98
Carlos Roberto Flores Facussé	1998—02
Ricardo Maduro Joest	2002—06

However, on June 28, 2009, President Zelaya was forced into exile by a military-backed coup. The coup occurred because of a disagreement between the president and his political opponents over changes he wanted to make to the Constitution through a referendum scheduled for June 28. The Honduran Congress, Supreme Court, and military all declared the planned poll illegal. Zelaya's opponents feared the changes to the Constitution would allow the sitting president to extend his presidency, which is unlawful under the current Constitution. The head of Congress, Roberto Micheletti, assumed the role of interim president of Honduras. Protesting Hondurans took to the streets, with groups for and against the coup. Although Zelaya maintained a great deal of international support, the new government blocked attempts for him to return.

Tropical storm Gamma killed more than 30 people and forced many thousands from their homes in November 2005, causing the greatest devastation since Hurricane Mitch.

GOVERNMENT

Supporters of Honduras's interim president, Roberto Micheletti, march in the capital city of Tegucigalpa.

THROUGHOUT ITS HISTORY Honduras has struggled to maintain political stability, and has often had a chaotic array of interest groups vying for influence. The military has seized power twice. However, in recent years, the political process has been more stable, and democratic elections have generally happened peacefully and openly. Honduras has five official political parties, and all these gained seats in the last elections in 2005.

A peace demonstration in Honduras. Freedom of speech is guaranteed by the Honduran constitution and includes the right to demonstrate.

NATIONAL GOVERNMENT

Honduras's national government is divided into three branches: executive, legislative, and judicial. Each branch is supposed to be autonomous, but in reality the executive branch dominates the legislative and judicial branches. There is also an elections tribunal, the National Elections Tribunal, which functions as an independent division with jurisdiction throughout the country.

The Casa Presidencial, or Presidential Palace, shows a strong Spanish colonial influence.

CONSTITUTION The present constitution of Honduras, the 16th since independence from Spain, was adopted on January 20, 1982, one week after almost 20 years of military rule ended. The Honduran constitution is seen more as a political ideal than a legal instrument, and has been changed in detail many times.

This constitution establishes three separate branches of government and provides for an independent elections tribunal that handles national elections. It also protects basic human rights, women's right to vote, child and labor rights, freedom of speech, freedom of the press, and issues of nationality, social security, health, education, and housing are dealt with in detail.

THE EXECUTIVE BRANCH is headed by the president, who is assisted by at least 12 cabinet ministers. The president is elected by a simple majority every four years and cannot run for a succeeding term.

The responsibilities of the president include organizing, directing, and promoting economic, education, health, and foreign policies. The president has the power to veto or approve laws approved by the National Congress with a few exceptions, such as constitutional amendments. The president is also given the military title of general commander.

THE LEGISLATIVE BRANCH consists of the unicameral National Congress—128 deputies are elected every four years at the same time as the president. The members are selected proportionally by administrative departments. The National Congress conducts legislative functions during regular annual sessions from January to October. Its roles are to approve choices of the president, appoint committees to study issues that come before the legislature, elect government officials, and approve the national budget, international treaties, and taxes.

THE JUDICIAL BRANCH of the government consists of the Supreme Court of Justice, courts of appeal, courts of first instance, and justices of the peace. The Supreme Court is a court of last resort. Fifteen judges are elected by the National Congress for a seven-year term. It has 14 constitutional powers and duties and is divided into three chambers—civil, criminal, and labor—with three justices assigned to each chamber. Courts of appeal have three-judge panels who hear appeals from all lower courts. The courts of first instance serve as trial courts for serious civil and criminal cases. Justices of the peace serve in each department of the country as investigators of minor cases.

THE NATIONAL ELECTIONS TRIBUNAL Since Honduras returned to civilian democratic rule in 1982, national elections have been held every four

Members of the Congress starting a session.

years to elect the president, the National Congress, and municipal officials. This tribunal is an independent body that is responsible for organizing and conducting elections. The National Registry of Persons works under the National Elections Tribunal and is responsible for issuing identity cards to all Hondurans (these are also voter registration cards) and conducting a census before each election.

LOCAL GOVERNMENT

Honduras is divided into 18 departments (provinces), which are subdivided into 298 municipalities (*municipios*). A municipality may include more than one city. There is also a Central District made up of Tegucigalpa and Comayagüela. The president freely appoints and removes governors for each department. Departmental governors are an extension of the executive branch of the national government. Each governor may freely appoint or remove a secretary to assist him or her. A municipality is administered by a mayor (*alcalde*) and a council elected every four years at the same time as the president. The council varies in size depending on the population of the municipality.

POLITICAL PARTIES

Two parties have traditionally been dominant—the Liberal Party of Honduras (*Partido Liberal de Honduras*—PLH) and the National Party of Honduras (*Partido Nacional de Honduras*—PNH). These were the only two official parties from 1902 to 1948, which laid the groundwork for the present-day system. The PLH was established in 1891 under the leadership of Policarpo Bonilla Vásquez and had its origins in the liberal reform efforts of the late 19th century. The PNH was formed in 1902 when a group broke off from the PLH. In 1963 it became aligned with the military.

Since the 1980s two small parties have emerged—the Innovation and Unity Party (*Partido Innovación y Unidad*—PINU) and the Christian Democratic Party of Honduras (*Partido Demócrata Cristiano de Honduras*—PDCH). They have participated in the national and legislative elections, but neither party has posed a threat to the political domination of the PLH and the PNH. More recently a leftist party, the Democratic Unification Party (*Partido Unificación Democrática*—PUD) emerged from four smaller parties in 1992. The PUD has contested elections since 1997 and holds five seats in the current National Congress.

ROLE OF THE MILITARY

Since the return to civilian democratic rule in 1982, the military's influence has been slowly receding. The military was a powerful force in domestic politics beginning in the 1950s. It controlled the presidency from 1963 until 1971. In 1972 the military took power again and kept it another 10 years. Today the workings of the two dominant parties appear to be free from military influence, although recent governments have sought military help in tackling the violent gang culture found in many of Honduras's cities.

There are few ideological differences between the Liberal Party and the National Party in Honduras, and allegiance to one group or the other is still often based on family tradition. The Liberal Party is stronger in urban areas and the more developed northern departments. The National Party, on the other hand, is stronger in more rural areas and the less developed southern agricultural departments.

Soldiers keeping the peace in Honduras despite the upheaval within and outside the country.

INTERNATIONAL RELATIONS

Since the 1980s Honduras has had a very tense relationship with its southern neighbor, Nicaragua. In the 1980s Nicaragua was governed by the left-wing Sandinistas, while Honduras's government and military were heavily backed by the United States, which opposed the Sandinistas. For many years one of the problems in this relationship was a disagreement over the two countries' maritime boundary in the Caribbean Sea. Both sides claimed fishing rights in the area and resorted to seizing each other's fishing vessels in the struggle for territory. However, in 2007, the dispute was settled by the ICJ to both countries' satisfaction.

POLITICS TODAY

The Liberal Party's Manuel Zelaya became president in 2006. Zelaya is a politician of great experience, having previously served in the government of Carlos Flores. Today Honduran politics is heavily influenced by a variety of special interest groups and political organizations. Such groups include business organizations such as the banana companies, labor and peasant groups—such as the Confederation of Honduran Workers (CTH) and General

U.S. president Barack Obama (*left*) shakes hands with Honduran president Manuel Zelaya Rosales (*right*).

The first women's group in Honduras was the Women's Cultural Society, formed in 1923. This group fought for economic and political rights for women. But it was not until 1955 that the fight for the right to vote was won. Honduras was the last Latin American country to give women suffrage. Women were also active in the formation of the labor movement and took part in the great banana strike of 1954. By the late 1980s women were represented at all levels of government, although their numbers were small. Women have held seats in the National Congress and the Supreme Court, high-level executive-branch positions, and mayorships, and both the National Party and the Liberal Party have supported women's nominations for presidential candidates.

VISITACIÓN PADILLA (1882–1960)

Padilla was a strong, ambitious, articulate woman in Honduras during the early 1900s. She started out as a schoolteacher and soon became Honduras's first female journalist. As a feminist she was certainly a pioneer in Central America and became the best-known feminist figure in Honduras. She felt it was important to draw women together to fight for what they believed in and what they needed. Padilla became president of the Women's Cultural Society, which led the struggle for women's economic and political rights. She also became involved in heated governmental politics, where she worked for peace during the troubled years of the early 20th century. In 1924 the United States was planning to send Marines into Honduras to help settle the political problems in Central America. Padilla cofounded the Boletin de Defensa Nacional, which led the protest against U.S. intervention.

A women's group was named after the Visitación Padilla Committee in honor of this impressive woman. The committee is dedicated to building a peaceful future for the children of Honduras.

Workers Confederation (CGT)—and popular, legally recognized groups—student, women's, human rights, and environmental groups. The government has started to hold the military accountable for human rights violations and has begun to root out corruption in government organizations.

ECONOMY

A worker unloads bananas in a market in Tegucigalpa.

CHAPTER 4

HONDURAS IS ONE OF the poorest developing countries in the Western Hemisphere, with a per head gross domestic product (GDP) of just $4,400 a year. Hondurans work under difficult conditions for very little income. The economy is divided geographically between the highlands and the lowlands. The people of the highlands contribute to the nation's economy mainly with subsistence farming, raising livestock, and mining. In the lowlands the chief occupations are in the plantations.

Honduras has historically had high inflation, with a rate of 12 percent recorded in 2008. This makes it difficult for Hondurans to gain any benefit from the growth of their economy and increases in pay.

Cattle grazing in La Lima. Raising livestock is a primary occupation in Honduras.

The most important economic centers are San Pedro Sula on the northern coast, which is highly industrialized, and Choluteca on the southern coast, which is a farming center for products such as shrimp, meat, and dairy produce.

The political turbulence that plagued Honduras and its Central American neighbors throughout the 1980s and 1990s negatively affected the Honduran economy, which is in need of capital and technical know-how. The economy was also greatly affected by the damage Hurricane Mitch did to important export crops in November 1998. More than 60 percent of that year's fruit crop was destroyed. It has taken Honduras a decade to rebuild its infrastructure and farming output. More recently the United States—Central America Free Trade Agreement (CAFTA) has helped foster investment from North America and has meant that Honduran goods can more easily be exported to American markets. However, growth remains dependent on the good health of the U.S. economy, its major trading partner, and on commodity prices, especially coffee.

A Honduran coffee farmer shows off his coffee beans.

EXPORTS

The economy of Honduras relies on two exports: bananas and coffee. Although Hurricane Mitch virtually wiped out the banana-growing industry in 1998, the industry had recovered to 60 percent of its pre-Mitch levels by 2000. Coffee beans account for over 20 percent of the country's export revenue. As with any developing country that depends on a few exports, the Honduran economy is at the mercy of world prices. However, the government is increasing its involvement in the economy and is diversifying exports in order to develop a more stable economy. Beef had the potential to become a very important export in the 1980s, but because of high production costs, the livestock industry now accounts for less than 3 percent of total exports, yet it is still an important export. Honduras also exports cotton, tobacco, pineapples, sugarcane, vegetables, and lobsters and shrimp. The United States is the destination of most Honduran exports.

PRIMARY OCCUPATIONS AND INDUSTRIES

The Honduran labor force is made up of mainly unskilled and uneducated laborers. More than half the rural population is landless and relies on seasonal labor paying low wages.

AGRICULTURE Because of the rugged, mountainous country, only 15 percent of the land in Honduras can be used for farming, yet agriculture employs 39.2 percent of the labor force and accounts for 13.4 percent of annual GDP. In the highlands and Pacific lowlands, ranching provides employment and livestock products for export. Large agribusinesses take up much of the arable highlands. The rest is divided between subsistence farmers, 55 percent of whom have less than 5 acres (2 hectares) of mediocre farmland and earn less than $2 a day, $500 per year, from those small plots. Over the past 20 years, the agricultural sector has lost about one-third of its earning power, largely because of a decline in prices for export crops, especially bananas and coffee.

Government statistics show that one-third of the workforce in Honduras is female and that many women run businesses. However, the vast majority of women are employed in menial, low-skill jobs.

Workers harvesting pineapples on a plantation in Honduras.

In the Caribbean coastal area, a different type of agriculture is practiced. Two large U.S. companies—Chiquita Brands International (formerly United Fruit Company) and Dole (formerly Standard Fruit and Steamship Company)—hold over half of the arable land. These companies produce a substantial part of the national income growing bananas and coffee beans for export.

FORESTRY Honduras was once famous for its mahogany trees, but now pine is the main commercial forest product. Because Honduras has extensive pine forests, forestry has the potential to contribute a large source of income. However, the country's forest has been heavily exploited. Large tracts have been cleared for agriculture, especially cattle ranches, and commercial timber exploitation has been inefficient. Many trees felled for lumber do not reach sawmills, and not all that do are processed.

FISHING is still a small industry, but it is developing along the Caribbean coast. The largest catch is of shrimp, most of which is exported to the United States.

Fishermen cast for wild shrimp in a lagoon in Honduras.

Workers in the Aquafinca Saint Peter fish-processing factory in Honduras. The company first started processing tilapia fish but is now also using the fish to produce biodiesel.

MINING produced the main exports in the late 1800s, but declined rapidly in importance during the 1900s. The largest mining company, the New York and Honduras Rosario Mining Company, produced $60 million worth of gold and silver from 1882 to 1954 before discontinuing most of its operations. Mining's contribution to the GDP declined steadily during the 1980s to account for only 2 percent of the GDP today. Yet Honduras remains the country richest in mineral resources in Central America. Gold, silver, lead, zinc, and cadmium are mined and exported to the United States and Europe.

MANUFACTURING employs roughly 20 percent of the workforce and accounts for roughly one-fifth of GDP. Food, drinks, textiles, clothing, chemicals, lumber, and paper products are the main goods manufactured and processed. Between 1990 and 1998, the number of workers in the sector grew from 9,000 to 120,000. A majority of these workers—70 percent—were women between the ages of 15 and 26. Manufacturing has attracted more foreign investment than any other industry in Honduras. Small Honduran shops make mostly clothing and food products, while Asian-owned textile industries have begun to dominate the smaller domestic manufacturing economy.

SERVICES Roughly 40 percent of the population of Honduras works in the service industry (including transportation and tourism) and services make up 59 percent of the country's income. Many Hondurans work as domestic help in the cities.

In the mid-1990s financial services in Honduras were opened up and the banking industry expanded rapidly. By the early part of the 21st century, financial assets in Honduras had been consolidated into the hands of a few large banks.

The ever-busy Puerto Cortes shipping port in Honduras.

TOURISM is one of the fastest-growing industries in Honduras. There are many beautiful natural attractions, most of them pristine and unspoiled. Foreigners come to Honduras to visit the Mayan ruins in Copán and the outstanding coral reef off the Bay Islands. Small ecotourism projects are considered to have significant potential, especially in the Bay Islands. More than a million tourist arrivals were recorded in Honduras in 2007, with more than 20,000 cruise-ship passengers visiting the country. In the same year tourism earned the country $567 million (up from $291 million in 2002).

ENERGY SOURCES

The Feria Centroamericana de Turismo y Artesanía, a Central American international tourism and crafts fair, is held annually from December 6 to 16 in Tegucigalpa.

For many years Hondurans have relied on fuelwood and biomass, mostly waste products from agricultural production, to supply them with energy. These sources have generally met approximately 50 percent of the country's total energy demand. Power from hydroelectric plants where rivers have been dammed provide almost half of Honduras's electricity. Honduran use of electricity is low but increasing: In urban areas more than 90 percent of the people have access to electricity, but in rural areas less than 50 percent of the people have access. Petroleum has never been produced in Honduras, so the country has relied on oil imports to fill much of its energy needs. A significant part of total export earnings are spent on purchasing oil.

TELECOMMUNICATIONS

Historically the telecommunications system in Honduras was outdated and poorly maintained. However, this has improved during the past decade. As of 2008 there were 821,200 lines in use across the country (roughly 1 per 10 people). Half the phones are in Tegucigalpa, a quarter are in San Pedro Sula, and the remainder are scattered all over the country in large towns. Internet use is low by the standards of developed countries, with 424,200 users recorded in 2007. However, more than 4 million Hondurans have cellular phones, or roughly half the population, as this is the cheapest and easiest way to make phone calls.

Television is popular, although there are not many channels. There are 11 television stations in the larger cities and 17 low-power transmitters in small towns. Radio is the primary mode of getting information to Hondurans. All parts of the country are in the range of at least one radio station. Many families sit around the radio in the evenings to listen to the news or stories.

People following a soccer game at a bar in Tegucigalpa.

A typical street scene in the cities of Honduras.

TRANSPORTATION

Because of the mountainous terrain, it has been difficult to create a transportation system to meet the entire country's needs. In 2000 Honduras had just over 8,451 miles (13,600 km) of roads, only 1,724 miles (2,775 km) of which were paved. Most of these roads connect the ports and industrial areas. Only one paved highway joins the Caribbean and the Pacific, passing through Puerto Cortés, San Pedro Sula, and Tegucigalpa. This major highway was badly damaged by Hurricane Mitch in November 1998, but it was the first road to be rebuilt. The Inter-American Highway (part of the Pan-American Highway) cuts across southern Honduras for about 100 miles (160 km). Other areas, served only by gravel and dirt roads that are often impassable during even moderately rainy weather, were accessible only by air after the hurricane. The government plans to pave many of these roads as they are reconstructed across Honduras.

The railroads were built by the original banana companies for transporting bananas to ports, not for transporting goods and passengers nationwide. Two rail systems provide freight and passenger service, and both are located in the north-central and northwestern coastal areas. Tegucigalpa remains the only Spanish-speaking capital in the Americas with no rail service whatsoever.

Four ports handle Honduras' seaborne trade—Puerto Cortés, Tela, La Ceiba, and Puerto Castilla. Most of the agricultural exports and imports of petroleum and manufactured products pass through Puerto Cortés.

Lack of alternative transportation through Honduras's mountains makes air travel important. There are four international airports—in Tegucigalpa, La Ceiba, Roatán and near San Pedro Sula. Domestic flights operate between the two cities and to Roatán. There is also air service to rural areas where planes land on small, unpaved fields.

WAGES

Each industry has its own minimum wage based on an eight-hour day shift. Overtime is paid for a shift of over eight hours, and the rate is higher if overtime hours occur during the night or are an extension of the night shift. In June each year workers receive a month's wages as a bonus for a full year's work.

In 2008 President Manuel Zelaya increased the minimum wage by 60 percent (from Lps [lempiras] 3,700 to Lps 5,500), raising monthly wages from $181 to $289. Although the new minimum wage was welcomed by many, some businesses have struggled to pay the higher costs and workers have been laid off as a consequence.

Laid-off workers protesting against the minimum wage ruling.

ENVIRONMENT

The reddish glow of twilight streams
into a resort on Roatán Island.

CHAPTER 5

ONDURAS HAS a diverse environment ranging from tropical islands and coastal mangroves to inland mountains and vast rain forests. The country is considered a biodiversity "hotspot" because of the numerous plant and animal species that can be found there, including endangered animals such as the jaguar, manatee, whale shark, and many rare species of turtles.

A margay cub roams freely in a nature reserve in Honduras. The margay is a spotted cat native to Central and South America.

Honduras has a number of thriving local conservation organizations. In 2005 Father Andres Jose Tamayo, a Honduran priest who established the Movement of Olancho—a green group that has fought illegal loggers—won the international Goldman prize for his environmental efforts in Honduras.

Leaded gasoline,
which causes
air pollution, has
been phased out in
Honduras. However,
for many years, the
law was ignored
by most Hondurans
and the authorities
rarely prosecuted
vehicles that used
leaded gas. In
recent years the
government has
sought to clamp
down on leaded
gasoline use, to a
great extent be-
cause of pressure
from local environ-
mental activists.

Today the country's main environmental issues are deforestation and soil erosion, both consequences of mining, logging, and land cultivation for farming. In recent years the Honduran government has sought to introduce pro-environmental legislation, but the biggest challenge is to help poor subsistence farmers exploit the forest in a responsible way. Although 75 percent of Honduras's rain forest is under government management, the government lacks funds to effectively manage the forest, and parks are understaffed.

DEFORESTATION

The Honduran rain forest is the largest north of the Amazon, consisting of 11,485,458.131 acres (4,648,000 ha), or 41 percent of the country's land. It is home to many species of animals. There are many protected biosphere reserves and national parks. Moskitia—the Mosquito coast—is one of Central America's few remaining areas of untamed wilderness. Huge expanses of untouched jungle are inhabited by small numbers of indigenous people, living a traditional lifestyle that has not changed in centuries. The area is home to a vast array of wildlife, including manatees, tapirs, crocodiles, toucans, macaws, and herons. However, in the Moskitia region, the Rio Platano Biosphere Reserve has suffered huge damage to its forests, due to increased farming and logging of its resources.

Brown pelicans nesting among red mangroves in the Bay Islands of Honduras.

Illegal logging is the main cause of deforestation in Honduras. By some estimates, as much as 85 percent of timber is harvested illegally. According to a 2005 investigation, the illegal timber trade feeds corruption among local government officials, politicians, police, and businesspeople, since so many people profit from the logging. According to some environmental organizations, Honduras suffered the greatest percentage loss of forest cover of any Latin American country during the past 20 years. Between 1990 and 2005, 37 percent of the country's forests disappeared, at a rate of more than 252,400 acres (102,143 ha) per year.

Smoke rising from a fire used to clear the pine forest areas for farmland in rural Honduras.

To a great degree Honduras's rapid deforestation is caused by the country's debilitating poverty, with poor subsistence farmers clearing forest to graze cattle, gather wood for fuel (65 percent of the country's energy comes from fuelwood), logging, and forest fires for the slash-and-burn method of farming. Forestry provides jobs for many thousands of Hondurans, and in a country where most of the population lives in poverty, the environment will always come second to people's livelihood. Increased government enforcement of logging laws are helping to limit the tree loss, but deforestation continues to deplete the country's forests.

Deforestation can also make the likelihood of mudslides much greater, as natural vegetation anchors the soil and reduces the amount of earth that can be easily washed away by rains and floods. Aerial surveys following Hurricane Mitch suggested that mudslides were worst in deforested areas.

Various hydroelectric projects have been planned in Honduras as a way of harnessing the power of Honduras's many mountain rivers and improving its inefficient energy supply. The latest, the Patuca River dam project, is still in the planning stages, but conservationists fear that the construction

and development of this massive dam will do untold damage to local protected rainforests, these include the Patuca National Park, the Tawhaka Asangni Biosphere Reserve, and the Rio Platano Biosphere Reserve.

MANGROVE FORESTS

Honduras has more native mangrove forest than any other country in Central America. The Honduran mangroves, which are found on both the Caribbean and Pacific coasts, are threatened with destruction by the shrimp industry, deforestation, and unsustainable building development. Local and international environmental groups are seeking to protect the environment of one of the largest areas of mangrove, the Gulf of Fonseca, by educating local fishermen to take advantage of the gulf's resources without harming the environment. By some estimates, the Gulf of Fonseca has lost about 40 percent of its original mangrove forests. If destruction continues at its current rate, Honduran mangroves will disappear by 2015.

Bottle-nosed dolphins swimming in the Bay Islands of Honduras.

ENDANGERED ANIMALS

Schools of whale sharks—the world's largest species of fish—can be found in the waters around the Bay Islands.

The International Union for Conservation of Nature (IUCN) lists one species of mammal as endangered and eight others as vulnerable in Honduras. The Roatán Island Agouti (a type of rodent) is considered endangered. The vulnerable animals include the American manatee, the Central American tapir, the giant anteater, the Honduran fruit-eating bat, the Honduran small-eared shrew, Van Gelder's bat, and the Jamaican Hutia, a tree- and cave-dwelling rodent. Even the country's national bird, the scarlet macaw (a type of parrot), is on the endangered list. The main threat to the animals is deforestation.

CLOUD FORESTS

As a mountainous land, Honduras has more "cloud forests" than any other Central American country. Cloud forests are areas of tropical forest at high altitude. Of the 13 national parks in Honduras, 12 include highland cloud forests. Cloud forests form a remarkable and unique ecosystem. At altitudes of 5,905 feet (1,800 m) or more, the clouds deposit tiny drops of water on the forest trees and plants, beginning a process called "'horizontal precipitation." Unlike lowland jungle, plants like bromeliads, orchids, clusia trees, and tree ferns can grow in cloud forests. Many mosses and other fungi

also thrive in the cooler, damp climate of these high-altitude forests. Although highly elusive, one of the most attractive residents of the cloud forest is the quetzal bird. There are large populations of this beautiful bird in Cusuco National Park, Pico Pujol, Sierra de Agalta, and La Muralla National Park. The cloud forests are also home to the blue morphos butterfly cougars, tapirs, sloths, and many species of monkeys.

The wildlife refuges of Punta Sal and the Laguna de Micos on the northern Caribbean coast are breeding grounds for shrimp, crabs, many types of fish, manatees, and dolphins. However, this makes them attractive to local fishermen, who have flouted the law in search of fish. One of the reasons for the decline of the manatee is the use of nets for fishing in rivers, estuaries, and the sea. It is estimated that there are only 400 to 700 manatees left in the Gulf of Honduras.

NATIONAL PARKS AND PROTECTED AREAS

Honduras has many protected areas and nature reserves, including government managed national parks, biosphere reserves, and wildlife refuges. More than a fifth of the country is designated reserve status. Some of the most important protected areas include the following.

CELAQUE MOUNTAIN NATIONAL PARK At 66,700 acres (27,000 ha), this is the third-largest protected area in Honduras, and one of the country's most impressive national parks. At its center is an outstanding cloud forest rich in animal species such as monkeys, tapirs, toucans, quetzals, jaguars, and deer.

CUERO Y SALADO WILDLIFE REFUGE Covering 33,000 acres (13,255 ha) and situated on the coast near la Ceiba, the reserve is named after the two local rivers, Cuero and Salado, that meet to form a large estuary. The park is home to rarely seen manatees, as well as howler and white-faced monkeys, sloths, agoutis, iguanas, and hundreds of bird species.

LANCETILLA BOTANICAL GARDENS Covering 3,165 acres (1,281 ha), this is the only botanical garden in Honduras and the second-largest botanical garden in the world. The gardens were established in 1926 by the Tela Railroad Company to experiment with growing various types of tropical plants. The gardens are home to numerous species of birds and the largest single collection of tropical fruit trees in the Western hemisphere. Many rare animals have also made their home here, such as the puma, howler monkey, wildcat, and deer.

Rio Cangrejal at the Pico Bonita National Park in Honduras.

LAGUNA DE BACALAR In 2003 this marine coastal wetland 18,271 acres (7,394 ha) was designated as a Wetland of International Importance. Located on the Caribbean coast, this marine wetland is characterized by broad-leaf forest, swamps, and mangrove forest. The area is also home to many endangered species such as the Caribbean manatee, rare birds such as the jabirus, and fish typical of this type of ecosystem, including the schoolmaster snapper and the horse-eye jack.

Children enjoying fresh water from a pump in Moskitia.

THE RIO PLATANO BIOSPHERE RESERVE This United Nations Educational, Scientific and Cultural Organization (UNESCO) World Heritage site is located in the region of Moskitia. At 1.297 million acres (525,000 ha), it is the largest park in Honduras. The reserve is an extremely diverse biosphere, and includes lagoons, coastal beaches, marshes, and pine forests. Animals that have made their home here include the green iguana, marine and sea turtles, white tail deer, and red deer.

WATER AND SANITATION

Although the water supply and sanitation has improved during the past decade, much of Honduras's sewage system is unreliable. Some rural areas still do not have any proper water supply, with villagers collecting water from local rivers, springs, and wells. Much of the water and sewage system was destroyed by Hurricane Mitch, and it has taken many years to repair the damage. Although the Honduran authorities have sought to improve the country's sewage system, there is little money available for such an expensive project. Honduras is not fully exploiting its water resources, with the inefficient sewage system, using only a fraction of the potential water available.

Honduran government data from 2006 suggest that 81 percent of homes have access to treated water and sanitation. However, World Health Organization (WHO) figures suggest that the average is closer to 75 percent, with 91 percent of urban homes being connected but only 62 percent of rural homes receiving water from the mains.

Water quality is poor by Latin American standards. In 2006 only 75 percent of the drinking water in urban areas was disinfected and 10 percent of the sewage received treatment. In rural areas the service is worst, with only a third of drinking water being treated. According to the WHO, most homes receive intermittent water supplies for an average of only 6 hours a day.

The quality of drinking water and inefficient sanitation is also a cause of disease and illness in Honduras, especially in rural areas. The rapid increase of the urban poor, as many Hondurans move from the villages to the towns and cities for work, has also put extra strain on urban sewerage systems. Waterborne disease such as hepatitis A and typhoid are still common in Honduras.

Scuba divers observe a hawksbill turtle feeding on the aquatic plants of Roatán Island.

WATER POLLUTION

Honduras's coastal mangroves and reed beds, waters, and reefs have also become affected by pollution, especially in recent years. The main causes of pollution in the marine environment are overfishing, poor sewage management, and pesticide run-off from farming. The coastal areas have also been put under tremendous pressure by the development of tourist facilities for the growing tourism industry.

The vast Mesoamerican barrier reef system runs off Honduras's Caribbean coast, close to the Bay Islands. It is part of the second-largest coral reef in the world, stretching from Honduras up to the Yucatan peninsula in Mexico, and home to many important marine species. Tourism, fishing, and

ECOTOURISM

In recent years ecotourism—people traveling to experience the wildlife and environment of a place—has grown in Honduras. Tourists mainly come from North America to visit the rain forest and to see native animals, such as the colorful parrots, iguanas, and turtles that inhabit this beautiful country. The Bay Islands are very popular dive sites, where hundreds of species of tropical fish and other marine animals live among the coral.

The government has attempted to expand the tourist industry through large-scale development projects. A plan emerged in the late 1990s to allow foreign nationals to own land and operate tourist-related businesses within 40 miles (64 km) of the coast. This plan was vigorously opposed by the coastal Amerindians who feared the development would disrupt their livelihoods and traditional way of life. Amerindians may be a minority in the overwhelmingly mestizo population, but they have made their voices heard in recent years. In 2000 the Honduran Congress rejected the measure that would have allowed foreigners to run tourist operations in the coastal regions. Clashes over coastal development between developers and indigenous groups will likely continue.

cargo ship traffic have all contributed to damaging the reef. However, local environmental groups, such as the Bay Islands Conservation Association, are working to protect and restore the reef. Based on methods tested in the Pacific, dying corals are planted and regenerated. Conservationists in the Bay Islands have also sought to nurture the local turtle population by protecting their nesting grounds. Turtles visit the islands every year from May until the end of October.

Mining has also caused water pollution in Honduras. The San Martin gold mine in the central Siria Valley region was first opened in 1999. Cyanide has been used there to extract the gold ore through "heap leaching," a method that percolates and separates the gold from the other metals. It is one of the cheapest and quickest ways to extract gold ore. However, local people have complained that the cyanide and arsenic have polluted local water supplies. In 2007 the mining company was fined by the government and ordered to mine in a way that complied with environmental regulations.

HONDURANS

Local schoolboys sitting on a colorful fountain in Honduras.

THE POPULATION OF HONDURAS was estimated to be 7,792,854 in 2009. Approximately 3.9 million Hondurans live in rural areas centered around small villages or towns, while 46 percent live in the cities. About 90 percent of the population is mestizo, people who are a racial mix of indigenous and European ancestry. The remaining inhabitants include indigenous peoples (7 percent), blacks from Africa and the Caribbean Islands (2 percent), whites who come mostly from Europe (1 percent), and a small number of immigrants from the Middle East.

According to a 2008 estimate, the average age of Hondurans was just 20.3 years old, meaning that the country has a very young population, with many more young people than old people.

ETHNIC GROUPS

Mestizos, whites, and most blacks are Ladino—people who speak Spanish and whose lifestyle follows Hispanic cultural patterns. Most Ladinos are members of the Roman Catholic Church. They range from poor subsistence farmers to businesspeople in the cities. Family is at the core of Ladino culture. These close family connections make it difficult for immigrants to penetrate Ladino culture, so different and separate subcultures of immigrants exist in the cities of Honduras. This lack of

ethnic mixing may seem surprising because almost all Ladinos themselves have a mixed racial ancestry. It is not that they are unfriendly. Ladinos simply value their extended families above all else, and so they remain tight-knit groups.

INDIGENOUS HONDURANS

Since colonial times there has been intermarriage between the native Hondurans and Spanish people. The remaining indigenous population consists of many different small groups who maintain customs set apart from Ladino culture.

Lenca women
in their brightly
colored dresses.

LENCA One of the largest remaining indigenous groups in Honduras is the Lenca, who are believed to have descended from the ancient Maya. Estimates suggest that there up to 100,000 Lenca, living mainly in the southwestern interior. Lenca women buy and sell vegetables in a market at La Esperanza-Intibucá and in Marcala.

The Lenca still practice some traditional customs. They cultivate communal lands instead of owning private plots and they use digging sticks instead of plows. Women wear long skirts and short blouses similar to those worn by women in colonial days. They usually work alongside the men in the fields. Other characteristics that set the Lenca apart are their festival dances, basket-weaving, pottery, and home brewing of the traditional liquor, *chicha*.

They have adopted some aspects of the Ladino national culture. The Lenca are Catholic, although they are more religious than the average Ladino, and they no longer speak their native language but instead speak dialects that have borrowed Spanish words. For these reasons there has been some debate as to whether the Lenca can be considered truly indigenous.

CHORTÍ INDIANS, another group with a Mayan heritage, live mostly near the town of Copán. Chortí villagers grow crops and trade in handicrafts. They are skilled makers of woven baskets, pottery, soap, wooden products, and leather goods.

JICAQUE In the past, northern indigenous groups were less settled than those living in the mountainous southwest. These groups were basically hunters and fishers. One northern group, the Jicaque (numbering roughly 8,600), once lived on the Caribbean coast until they were driven inland by colonists, where they began to settle and cultivate corn like the western Indians. Only a few hundred maintain their language and traditions. They dress in old-style tunics. Their homes are distinctive, made of planks tied with vines and roofed with thatch. They still hunt with blowguns.

Two Miskito Indian boys pose happily by a boat.

MISKITO The Miskito Indians are an isolated group who live harmoniously on the Mosquito Coast in northeastern Honduras. The area was essentially ignored by the Spanish, so the Miskito were left to themselves, more so than the rest of the people of Honduras. They are related to other Miskito Indian groups in South America with whom they share a similar language. They number approximately 40,000 people.

There has been intermarriage between the Miskito and blacks, often escaped slaves who sought the north coast for refuge. The Miskito today are a racially mixed population of indigenous, African, and European origin, mostly British. Many still speak a Creole language with contributions from Spanish, English, and German. They are generally considered indigenous.

Miskito cultivate yucca, beans, and corn in shifting agriculture. They burn and clear plots, then move on when the land is exhausted, leaving it to replenish itself. They also raise livestock such as chickens, pigs, and cows.

Because the Miskito live on the coast and rely on waterways for transportation, they have developed their own style of dugout and flat bottom boats. Fishing is important to their livelihood. Some Miskito stun their catch with arrows poisoned with an extract from jungle vines.

CHOROTEGA, PIPIL, PAYA, AND PECH These other indigenous groups number only a couple of hundred people. The Chorotega migrated from Mexico in pre-Columbian times and have retained many of their religious and cultural traits. The Pipil, who are of Nahuatl descent, live along the southwestern mountain slopes.

The exact origin of the Paya is unknown, but their ancestors are believed to have come from South America. They live in the lush and humid river regions of the Mosquito Coast, many near the Río Plátano, working as subsistence farmers and fishermen. They use farming tools, fishing poles, and spears that they make themselves.

The Pech, another indigenous group of the Mosquito Coast, are believed to be descendants of the Paya. Today their population has been reduced to fewer than 2,500. The Pech men fish, and women tend to crops and livestock. Pech children now go to Pech schools during the day but still help their parents before and after school.

A boy from the rapidly dwindling Pech indigenous group in Honduras.

BLACKS

Two distinct groups of blacks have settled in Honduras: the Black Carib, known as the Garifuna, and the black population in the Bay Islands.

The Black Carib settled in coastal villages along the Caribbean coast in the early 1800s. They are descendants of freed African slaves who were deported by the British in 1797 from the island of Saint Vincent in the Caribbean. They speak a Carib-based Creole that mixes English with local languages.

The Black Carib share many customs with the Miskito Indians. Both groups have been self-sufficient through farming and fishing for generations, but today, many of the men have to work outside the region to supplement an income that has been reduced by a loss of land. Many families are split up for long periods of time.

Many of the population on the Bay Islands are of mixed race. These people have descended from English-speaking blacks and whites from Belize and the Cayman Islands. Their traditions are distinctly West Indian and they speak Creole or Caribbean English.

Women from the Garifuna, (Black Carib) community in Honduras.

ARABS

There is a thriving Arab community in Honduras descended from immigrants who arrived in the early 1900s, mostly from Palestine and Lebanon. The Arabs have remained culturally distinct by keeping many of their own traditions alive. They were first successful as merchants and then moved to the industrial cities where they have become economically quite powerful.

SOCIAL HIERARCHY

Honduras is one of the poorest countries in the Western Hemisphere, with wealth very unevenly spread: The top 10 percent of the population controls more than 40 percent of the country's wealth. The majority of the Hondurans are poverty-stricken subsistence farmers, hired hands on large corporate farms, and poorly paid laborers in the cities. Since the 1950s, however, a small middle class has also emerged. There is little social conflict between the classes, but the increasing poverty of the majority and an increase in the wealth and power of the upper class has long been a concern.

Both the Paya and the Pech are proud people with fascinating customs, skills, and knowledge. From the forest and river they get food, shelter, and medicine, and fulfill their every other need. In return, they conserve and protect the forest and river as their ancestors have done for hundreds of years.

UPPER CLASS The Honduran elite is divided into two basic groups—the traditional elite, who were originally owners of large rural estates, and the military elite. The traditional elite were *hacendados* (hah-sen-DAH-dohs), the owners of large haciendas in the interior highlands and valleys. Many still live on their estates. After World War II, this group of wealthy landowners became involved in cattle production in response to the increase in the beef market. However, the land they used for cattle ranching— ultimately to export food to other countries—had originally been used for domestic food production. Therefore, social tensions increased in rural Honduras between the upper and lower classes.

This group of wealthy people is not particularly cohesive. They have different interests when it comes to political and economic issues. Many of them also have competing businesses. Politically there are as many Conservatives as there are Liberals. Some Liberals support and work toward the social change that middle and lower classes have sought over the years.

The military elite emerged in the mid-1950s when the armed forces underwent a major transformation. The military developed from being a variety of provincial militia groups to a United States—trained national institution. Because the traditional elite did not favor this military institution, the two groups have remained distinct. Possibly as a result of this separation of interest between the two elite groups, neither has become overwhelmingly powerful.

MIDDLE CLASS The small group that makes up the middle class is growing at a steady pace and is mostly settled in the cities. People who are considered middle-class are those with a higher education—college students, professors, teachers, civil servants, engineers, and merchants. On the Caribbean coast, the growth of the middle class was directly related to the area's industrial and business enterprises. In the north the success of merchants was due to

Children from upper- and middle-class Honduran families dress much like children in urban Western societies.

the market demands created by employed workers in the area's agribusiness. Although the middle class makes a decent income compared with the lower class, their income is still low by North American standards.

Banana plantation workers riding to their work.

This group is still small because although the growth in industry and commerce has improved in the last decade, it has still been slow by world standards. Job opportunities are scarce, but many people move to the cities every year seeking to end their poverty and live a middle-class lifestyle. Many middle-class citizens are involved in the politics of social change. They create and join unions, church groups, and other political organizations.

LOWER CLASS The lower class is divided into two groups based on where they live. Traditionally the poor people of Honduras have been the peasants in rural areas, but there is a growing lower class in the cities. Peasants are subsistence farmers called campesinos who make a living off their land.

Today, because so much land has been absorbed by commercial agribusiness, family subsistence off the land is difficult. This situation began after the 1950s when cattle and cotton production for export increased, and land was absorbed to become part of large agribusinesses. When the small plots of land were no longer enough to support the family, people either went to work on nearby large farms or migrated to the cities in search of employment.

The urban poor now consists of many of the campesinos who moved to cities looking for employment opportunities. This has created a very large population of impoverished, unemployed people looking for work and living on the streets in cities such as Tegucigalpa and San Pedro Sula. Many of those who do find work end up employed in the service industry, doing domestic work such as cleaning the homes of the wealthy. Some join the construction industry, while others join the assembly lines that manufacture products such as shoes, clothing, baskets, and furniture.

POPULATION CHANGES

Modern women from the Garifuna community standing in front of a shop in Honduras.

In the second half of the 20th century there has been a major increase in the population, but the population density is still relatively low. Birth rates are high by developed countries standards, with an average of 3.27 children being born to each woman in 2008. It is estimated that the population in 2015 will be at least 8.8 million. There has been significant immigration from neighboring Central American countries that have had higher levels of civil conflict. The growth of the banana industry resulted in the first major shift in population. In the early 1900s many Hondurans moved to the Caribbean coast to seek employment on the plantations. Today most internal migration is from rural areas to urban centers, especially the two largest cities, Tegucigalpa and San Pedro Sula. In the 1950s Tegucigalpa's population increased by 75 percent, causing inadequate housing and the emergence of shantytowns.

Most migrants today are in their teens or early twenties, and they seek a better standard of living beyond the poverty of farm life. Honduran men tend to move from their family land to wherever there is a developing agricultural area or to cities for work in artisan shops or as laborers in factories or construction. Women, on the other hand, have a limited choice when it comes to employment. Most migrant women are those who want to escape economic hardship and early marriage and motherhood. These women end up in the cities working as domestic help for the elite, in factories, or as street vendors.

Most towns have folk dance groups that wear traditional dress. A common style, originally worn by the Lenca, is all white for men and women. The white, flowing cotton material called manta was once worn mainly by the poor, but its use has spread widely. This style of dress is considered most appropriate for dancing Lenca and mestizo dances with indigenous influences. It is also the most common clothing for typical dolls in the central region. Another very popular folk dance dress is that found in the La Paz department. Women's dresses are very brightly colored and often have shiny metallic decorations or colored ribbons that flutter as the women dance.

DRESS

Hondurans value physical appearance, and they dress formally and neatly. Ladinos wear Western-style clothes. Women usually wear a colorful dress or a skirt and blouse, while men wear long-sleeved dress shirts and slacks. Wearing jeans with a T-shirt is considered too informal, especially outdoors in Tegucigalpa or San Pedro Sula. Children always wear uniforms to school. Public school children wear white and blue. Private schools have their own colored uniforms. The cities can look very colorful when school lets out, with all the children wearing various color clothing.

Indigenous groups each have their own traditional dress. They wear clothing that varies from completely traditional dress to a mixture of Western and traditional styles.

Honduras has a wide variety of traditional folk dance costumes and many are still worn on special occasions such as the celebration of a town's patron saint's day. The Honduran post office once issued a series of stamps showing traditional dress from different parts of the country.

Schoolboys in their uniforms on the eastern Caribbean coast of Honduras.

LIFESTYLE

Locals walking down a cobbled street in Copán.

HONDURAS HAS TRADITIONALLY been a farming society, and in spite of recent urban growth, it is still one of the least urbanized countries of Central America. The poor rural living conditions are of special concern, as the people are malnourished and are perpetually struggling to make ends meet.

In 1990 roughly 44 percent of Hondurans lived in towns and cities. By 2010 the number is expected to reach 59 percent. This rapid move from the country to the towns and cities has placed great pressure on Hondurans' traditional sense of community, with greater numbers of people competing for fewer jobs. Yet families provide an important support system that keeps Hondurans relatively content. They help one another, creating a real sense of community.

FAMILY ROLES

The family is the cornerstone of Honduran society and culture. Extended families are close-knit, often living in one home, including not only grandparents, but also aunts, uncles, and cousins. The closest relationships are usually familial ones, and any leisure time, such as celebrating festivals, is spent with relatives. Children are taught from a young age that relatives are to be trusted above everyone else. Families provide important social support, especially for women. And when men go into business, it is usually with other family members.

Thousands of Hondurans—especially young men—leave the country each year, most of them to find better-paid work in the United States. The money sent home by the overseas workers is an important source of income for many families.

A discrepancy exists, however, between this ideal of family and some Honduran families. Marriage is expensive, so many couples live together but are not legally married. Many men abandon their wives, girlfriends, and children, especially in the cities. Many households are run by single mothers, especially in Tegucigalpa. Honduran society disapproves of a man who does not support his children. Despite this some men do not assume the responsibilities of fatherhood.

MEN The concept of machismo is evident throughout all socioeconomic levels. Men are expected to be macho—daring, strong, unemotional, and brave. Men prove their masculinity or machismo by flirting with women, being demanding, and acting in an aggressive way. Boys are encouraged from an early age to act freely, and mostly do not help out around the house. Effeminate behavior is usually ridiculed in a country where macho values hold sway.

The father's role varies depending on the family, but generally fathers must be respected and obeyed. They are more removed from daily family affairs but usually have the final say in important matters. Men often do not feel a responsibility for their children, expecting women to take care of them completely. Men run the farms or send money home if they are working elsewhere.

This rural Honduran man works on a tobacco plantation to support his family.

WOMEN The female ideal of *marianismo* (mah-ree-ahn-EEZ-moh) is to be loyal, chaste, and submissive. Girls are encouraged to be more emotional and more vulnerable. Women are supposed to take care of their husbands or boyfriends and their children. However, Honduran women are strong and capable. They often work in the fields alongside men, as well as work in the kitchen.

More women are getting a higher education today, but those who do are still paid less than men for the same kind of work. Grandmothers and aunts often take care of the children so that a young mother can work outside the home or go to school.

CHILDREN are valued, honored, and cherished. They are expected to work hard at home and at school, but they are pampered as well. Generally speaking, children are valued as the next generation, and parents want their children to be better educated and have more money than they did.

However, this ideal is not completely followed in poverty-stricken families. Children of such families are often not pampered at all, and they are sometimes ignored. Men who permanently leave their families often do not send money to their wives or girlfriends in order to provide for their children. When a woman has children from a previous relationship, they may not be cared for by her new husband or boyfriend, as they are not his own.

Young boys and girls are treated very differently. Boys can run around unsupervised, while girls are expected to be quiet and helpful. Girls are carefully groomed and chaperoned. They are expected to be virgins when they marry and are vigilantly guarded against immoral conduct.

ELDERS Grandparents almost always live with their families. They are held in high regard and are viewed as a source of wisdom. They are treated and spoken to with the utmost respect. However, grandparents rarely get very old, unless they come from a wealthy family, due to the lack of proper food and health care. Poverty and old age are rarely seen together and elders work as long as they are able. For them, there is no such thing as retirement.

A girl does the family's laundry. Little girls are encouraged to help their mothers and families both within and outside the home.

LIFE CYCLE EVENTS

A typical Honduran wedding. After the ceremony, which takes place in a Catholic church, the bride's family usually holds an elaborate fiesta at their home, with refreshments and dancing.

BIRTH Women accept pregnancies with joy even though they may not be able to afford to have children. Women in rural areas do not have hospitals to go to for childbirth, so birthing takes place at home with the help of the town's midwife, or simply other women in the family. Godparents are chosen and children are baptized in a Catholic church as soon as a priest is in town, which may not be until the next festival. If this is the case, many babies are baptized on the same day and a large town party may follow afterward.

PUBERTY Children receive confirmation in a Catholic church when they are in their early teens. It is a time for all the relatives to celebrate. By this age, children have already taken on many responsibilities in the household or are working outside the house to earn money.

COURTSHIP AND MARRIAGE It is taboo for two teenagers to go on a date without a chaperone. If a date is arranged, sometimes the girl's whole family will go along. In this case, the boyfriend is expected to pay for the whole family. Because of widespread poverty, young Hondurans cannot afford to date often, and marriages often take place after very little courtship.

Marriages, especially in rural areas, are often common-law because religious marriages are expensive and there may not be a residential priest. Some couples get a civil marriage, which is less expensive and makes it easier to get a divorce should things not work out. Middle- and upper-class couples usually have religious marriages with a formal engagement.

DEATH A Catholic funeral is very important in Honduras. The funeral service in church is followed by nine days of mourning at the deceased person's home. This practice is repeated on the death anniversary.

RURAL LIFESTYLES For campesinos, or peasants, who live in the mountains, work is difficult and is never over. But however busy or tired they are, rural people are often smiling and laughing at stories they share with one another. If they need to travel somewhere, such as the market, they go on foot, often spending the greatest part of their day walking.

A campesina wakes up at 5:00 A.M. and begins work in the kitchen. If she has daughters, they will get up and help, too. Women spend the day making tortillas for their families. They boil, wash, and grind the corn to make coarse corn flour. They also bake bread, preserve fruit, wash clothes by hand, clean the house, and feed the chickens and cows. Mothers of infants tend to the babies, while older girls spend much of their time looking after younger siblings.

Campesinos often wake up as early as 3:00 A.M. with their sons. They head out to the fields to plant, tend crops, or harvest. They use hoes, machetes, and digging sticks, and carry loads such as sacks of seed on their backs. Boys will receive their own plot of land to be responsible for at a young age—at 14, if they have been going to school. Children often have the job of scaring birds from cornfields with slingshots, fetching water, and carrying a hot lunch from home to their fathers and older brothers in the field.

Farmers use the traditional slash-and-burn method. Every two years families move to a new plot of land when the soil they have been farming has lost all its nutrients. They clear the land by slashing the growth down to the ground, then burning away the rest. Today farmers are being taught soil conservation techniques such as terracing so that they will be able to farm one piece of land much longer.

These Honduran children stand by the gravestone of their grandmother.

Some campesinos also spend a part of their week squeezing sugarcane for juice to make sugar blocks to sell. Many campesinos are forced to find part-time work away from home to supplement their incomes, as there is not enough land for all of them.

MARKETS Some families spend much of their time growing or making things to sell at the market. The families that do not live in a town with a market will load a small cart with their merchandise, which is then pulled by the family cow. Hondurans may walk up to 20 miles (32 km) over mountain ranges without any paths to get to a market. At the market some women carry handmade baskets filled with flat breads on their heads as they look for buyers. Men and women work stalls where people come to barter over merchandise. They sell vegetables, fruit, bread, and chickens, as well as handmade straw hats, baskets, wooden statues of saints, vases, and toys.

HOUSING Families live in tiny rural towns, sometimes as small as a dozen dwellings clustered near a rundown church, which often doubles as a one-room schoolhouse as well. The homes are one- or two-room huts made from

Suburban houses on a hill in the capital city of Tegucigalpa.

clay, adobe, or rough-hewn, unpainted boards and have palm leaf roofs and bare dirt floors. In rural areas few people can afford proper furniture for their basic homes. Electricity, refrigeration, and running water are very rare. Water must be carried by mule or cow from the nearest streams, sometimes miles away.

URBAN LIFESTYLES

Compared with campesinos, urban residents live in comfort, although by Western standards, there are few conveniences available. Families still live together and everyone who is old enough to work adds to the family income. Very few Hondurans can afford a car or the expensive imported gasoline it runs on. Most people travel by taxi or bus—both are affordable and comfortable.

The men who work in the cities of Tegucigalpa, San Pedro Sula, Puerto Cortés, and La Ceiba are often skilled workers who went to a trade school, and a few to a university. The head of the household, as well as any older sons, may be a mechanic, construction worker, furniture repairman, or an attendant at a filling station. With the influx of foreign investment during the past decade, many men also work in industries producing auto parts and machinery, safety and security equipment, building products, and electrical machinery. Some men may own a small business with their brothers or cousins. After work they may stop to have a few drinks with other men before returning home.

The women who work in the cities are often teachers, secretaries, or domestic workers. During the past decade larger numbers of women have moved into the manufacturing industries, working in clothing factories, food processing, and drinks industries. Women are responsible for cleaning, laundry, and cooking in their own homes in addition to working outside the home all day.

HOUSING A family in the city can usually afford a small home with an open patio and a red-tiled roof. Many people live in one-room apartments. Some homes have a small kitchen as well. The family traditionally gathers around the kitchen table at the end of the day to discuss events and share stories.

A Family Code passed in 1984 gave more rights to single mothers, requiring divorced men to help in the rearing of their children. However, despite these legal rights, in rural areas it is rare for mothers to receive any form of child support from children's fathers.

EDUCATION

The educational system in Honduras is one of the least developed in Central America. United Nations statistics show that barely 32 out of every 100 students finish primary school without repeating grades. Public education is free and obligatory for every Honduran child from age 7 to 14, but not every child receives this benefit. Many students, especially in rural areas, go to school for grades one and two and then leave school to work and help earn a living for the family, usually by helping out on the farm. Nevertheless this is a major improvement for before the education reforms of 1957 there was no national education system, and education was the privilege of those wealthy enough to send their children to private institutions. In practice this is still relatively true because of the shortage of schools and teachers, the poor wages and training of teachers, and the high cost of materials needed for public schools. The wealthy send their children to private schools where there are better-educated and better-paid teachers, as well as more money for school supplies.

Students in a lecture at Tegucigalpa University.

All schools are supported by the Catholic Church and catechism is taught in class. Schools in the cities are commonly divided into boys' and girls' schools.

There is typically only one teacher, usually female, for grades one and two. In most public schools, the teacher may have as many as 80 students in her classroom. Grades three to six also have one teacher per classroom. There are fewer students in the higher grades but they are still too many for one teacher to give significant time and attention to each individual.

HIGHER EDUCATION After completing grade six, a small number of students continue their education. Grades seven to nine are considered "college," or secondary school. Here students have a different teacher for each subject.

A RURAL SCHOOL DAY

Students wake as early as 3:00 A.M. to do chores before school—boys out on the farm, girls in the kitchen. They then walk to school, often a few miles. Classes start around 8:00 A.M. and go on until noon, when it starts to get hot. When students arrive at school they usually get a free meal. This is very often the most nutritious meal they will eat all day. In primary (elementary) school a regular class will be taught Spanish vocabulary, and then students read or write a story using the new vocabulary. Primary school students also learn farming techniques. Each class has its own plot of land where students grow beans and corn. Subjects in grades three to six include history, politics, mathematics, and science. At recess, girls sing and dance in large groups. Older boys play soccer. After school and the long walk home, children do more chores.

Grades 10 through 12 are called trade schools, or technical schools. Students who complete trade school may then become teachers, computer technicians, carpenters, and so on. Many women aspire to become teachers.

There are a few universities in Honduras, and less than 8 percent of children enrolled at primary level continue to university-level education. The National Autonomous University of Honduras (Universidad Nacional Autónoma de Honduras—UNAH) is the main school of higher learning. Located in Tegucigalpa, the UNAH was founded in 1847 and became an autonomous institution in 1957. The university also has branches in San Pedro Sula and La Ceiba.

Hondurans go to college to become doctors, lawyers, professors, and engineers. More and more women go to college today.

LITERACY

In Honduras 80 percent of the population was considered to have reached a basic level of literacy by age 15, according to a census carried out between 2000 and 2004. Illiteracy rates vary depending on where Hondurans live. In rural settlements, especially in the western sections, more than 80 percent of the people cannot read and write. In the highlands near the capital and in the cities along the northern coast, illiteracy is much lower. The government is attempting to combat illiteracy, but because it is difficult to enforce the compulsory education law in remote areas, progress has been slow.

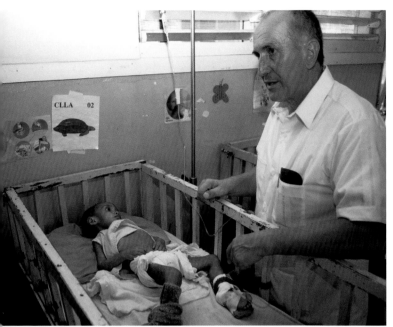

A doctor caring for a sick child in the children's ward of a hospital in Honduras.

HEALTH AND WELFARE

The quality of health care and access to it vary depending on location and income levels. In rural areas access to trained medical personnel is limited, and in isolated regions there are almost no doctors. Rural inhabitants have to travel to Tegucigalpa or San Pedro Sula to receive quality medical care, but the cost of care and travel prevent many Hondurans from getting proper treatment.

The lack of medical care for the majority of Hondurans is apparent in their poor health. Poverty also imposes restrictions on the food they eat, so malnutrition is widespread, causing many young children to have stunted growth. According to the WHO, three-quarters of Hondurans lack proper vitamins for good health. A basic diet of corn, beans, and rice—which is the staple for most poor, rural Hondurans—does not cover all their dietary and health needs. In 2009 the infant mortality rate was estimated to be 24 deaths per 1,000 live births—an improvement over previous years, but still high. Average life expectancy in 2009 was estimated to be 68 for men and 71 for women.

Most of the population lacks access to running water and sanitation facilities. Infectious and parasitic diseases are the leading causes of death. Diseases caused by poor sanitation and poor water quality include bacterial diarrhea, hepatitis A, and typhoid. Alcoholism and drug addiction are also common health problems. In the cities there has been a dramatic rise in human immunodeficiency virus (HIV) infections that cause acquired immune deficiency syndrome (AIDS), with 1,900 deaths recorded in 2007. The disease is spreading through intravenous drug use and prostitution.

Hurricane Mitch brought further health-related problems to the country in November 1998. Water contaminated by widespread death and destruction carried deadly diseases such as malaria and cholera. International relief

CHAGAS DISEASE

Insects are a common cause of disease in Honduras. About 600,000 Hondurans are affected by Chagas disease, which usually starts with a high fever and swelling of the eyelids on the side of the face near the bite wound. Later in life the disease can reappear and attack vital organs, such as the heart and colon. The disease is spread by chinches, blood-sucking bugs, which tend to attack their victims at night, transmitting the parasite Trypanosomoa cruzi. Chagas disease mainly affects the rural poor. A study found that the traditional Lenca homes made of mud walls and thatched roofs were ideal shelters for the Chagas-spreading bugs. Keeping animals inside the home also contributed to the spread of the disease.

International aid agencies, such as Canadian International Development Agency (CIDA) and Pan American Health Organization, have been involved in treating tens of thousands of Honduran homes with anti-bug sprays, as well as treating children against the disease. In one rural area, (San Francisco de Opalaca), government and international agencies built new homes made from adobe brick walls, cement floors and zinc sheet roofs—which do not attract insects. By 2007, more than 90 percent of the Chagas sufferers treated in this area had been cured. If a similar building and treatment program could be applied across the country, the disease would soon be eradicated, but such projects are expensive and difficult to implement in Honduras's isolated rural communities.

brought in water purification machines and vaccinations against such diseases to help keep down the spread of fatal illnesses. Thousands suffered from respiratory illnesses, including pneumonia, after the rains.

HEALTH PERCEPTIONS Most Hondurans do not relate their health problems to their real causes, for example, to malnutrition or environmental hazards. When a state of affairs has existed for generations—there has not been a dramatic food shortage, for example, but the diet has been continually inadequate—people fail to make the connection between poor diet and poor health. Their long-term poverty also means they have few options. Stunted children, infectious diseases, mental retardation, constant tiredness, and low productivity are viewed as normal because they have been the norm for centuries. Many Hondurans have never known what a healthy, nourished, comfortable life feels like.

RELIGION

The exquisite Delores Church in central Tegucigalpa.

THE HONDURAN CONSTITUTION guarantees religious freedom and the separation of the church and the state. Although more than 80 percent of the population is officially recognized as Roman Catholic, recent surveys suggest that a quarter of this number identifies with the more newly established evangelical Protestant churches.

However, many Hondurans, especially in remote areas, have mixed their primary Christian religion with ancient indigenous ceremonies, superstitions, and magic.

Catholic crucifixes for sale in Copán.

Catholics receiving
Holy Communion
at the San Miguel
Archangel cathe-
dral in Tegucigalpa.

CATHOLICISM

The Spanish brought the Roman Catholic faith to Latin America over 450 years ago. Many Hondurans are culturally Catholic rather than practicing Catholics. Catholic baptisms, first communions, weddings, and funerals are very important events that celebrate milestones in people's lives.

However, during the past three decades, the Catholic Church has been expanding the influence of Catholicism to enfold daily living and participation. The Church is also trying to recruit more Honduran-born clerics. Of the 381 priests working in Honduras today, only a minority are native Hondurans.

INCREASING RELIGIOUS ACTIVITIES In the 1950s and 1960s priests and nuns were sent to Honduras from around the world to build churches and evangelize in order to increase Catholic membership and activities. These missionaries found Honduras to be a country of mainly devout people who had as much belief in superstition and magic as in church dogma.

The Catholic Church reached out to the rural areas where poverty and illiteracy were widespread. It tackled these socioeconomic problems by introducing literacy and social service programs. With the creation of church groups such as the Christian Movement for Justice, the Catholic Church has taken on an important social role in Honduran society. Catholic schools receive government subsidies, and religious instruction is a part of the public school curriculum.

THE CULT OF THE SAINTS Hondurans believe in the power of Catholic saints. In each Catholic home, there is a picture or statue of a particular saint, very often the Virgin Mary. People pray to the saints for intervention or protection in their lives. Other popular saints are ones that are believed to offer protection on given occasions, such as traveling, or that bless a particular situation, such as the health of infants and children. Hondurans also make pilgrimages to pray to certain saints during particular festivals or occasions. Some people promise to make a pilgrimage if a certain prayer is answered. Pilgrimages to the Basilica of the Virgin of Suyapa near Tegucigalpa and to Esquipulas in Guatemala are made by the faithful.

The Black Carib people, or the Garifunas, still maintain their own religious system. It is a mixture of African and Amerindian traditions, but includes Catholic elements. The Garifunas consider dreams and possession rituals important ways of accessing their spiritual consciousness.

A Catholic home altar decorated with flowers, drapery, candles, and religious statues.

The Virgin of Suyapa is the well-loved patron saint of Honduras.

THE VIRGIN OF SUYAPA

Outside Tegucigalpa, in a place called Suyapa, is one of Central America's most impressive religious shrines, the Basilica of the Virgin of Suyapa, the patron saint of Honduras and all Central America. The statue, also known as Our Lady of Suyapa, is the country's most popular religious image, and the focus of a large annual pilgrimage. The small 18th-century statue of the Virgin is believed to have miraculous healing powers. The statue is honored inside the massive basilica, which is decorated with magnificent stained glass windows and a marble altar with bronze and gold designs. The Fair of the Virgin of Suyapa takes place every year throughout Honduras from February 3 to 10. This fair is one of Honduras's most important holidays. Many thousands of people from all over Central America make pilgrimages to visit the statue on her name day, February 3, a commemoration of the day she was found.

SACRAMENTS Hondurans begin their introduction to the Catholic religion by being baptized. If a small town does not have its own priest, it is customary to wait for a fiesta (celebration) when a priest will come to celebrate the festival and, at that time, perform all the town's baptisms at once. A fiesta usually follows a baptism and the whole extended family attend.

The Virgin of Suyapa was declared the patron saint of Honduras by Pope Pius XII on April 25, 1953.

After a Catholic marriage ceremony, where there is an exchange of rings and vows, a fiesta is held in the home of either the bride or groom's parents—usually at the house of whomever is wealthier. After food and drink at the house, the celebration shifts to a larger hall for a dance if the budget allows.

Catholic funerals are absolutely traditional within Catholic families. Immediately after death, the family holds a novena, or nine nights of prayer in front of the saint's altar at home. Novenas are also often held six months after the death and on its first anniversary. Close friends and family are invited to novenas.

PROTESTANTISM

Evangélicos (eh-van-HAY-lee-kohs) are Protestant groups that have emerged as important religious forces since the 1980s. They sponsor many social service programs that receive much of their funding from the United States.

The National Basilica Catholic church in Tegucigalpa.

Few Hondurans who profess to be evangelicals belong to the mainstream Protestant denominations, such as Lutheran. Today the largest evangelical churches in the country are the Methodists, the Southern Baptists, the Central American Mission, the Abundant Life Church, and the charismatic Pentecostal denomination, the Assemblies of God.

The largest population of Protestants is made up of the English-speaking inhabitants of the Bay Islands. This geographical religious split is due to the fact that the British were the main influence in the Bay Islands, not the Roman Catholic Spanish who ruled the mainland.

PLACES OF WORSHIP

Places of worship in Honduras include Catholic and Protestant churches that vary from extravagant, ornate basilicas presided over by a bishop to meager, thatched-roof buildings in small towns, with no priests at all. Paintings and statues of saints decorate the Roman Catholic churches regardless of the town's wealth.

Catholics may go to church to pray to a saint different from the one they venerate in their own home. Masses are held on Sundays, mostly in Spanish, but there are services in English in the larger cities.

The Protestant evangelical churches are newer and simpler in style, reflecting their belief that the church is made of people, not walls. English services are more common in evangelical churches due to the British and American influence in the spread of the Protestant faith.

A Catholic family saying grace before their meal.

OTHER RELIGIONS

The immigrant population accounts for the presence of other religions in Tegucigalpa and San Pedro Sula. They include Judaism (Jews), Church of Jesus Christ of Latter-Day Saints (Mormons), and Mennonite Protestantism. There are also a few indigenous tribal religions, as well as some African religious traditions practiced by the Black Carib on the north coast. Recently a temple of the Church of Jesus Christ of Latter-Day Saints has been planned for the growing Seventh-Day Adventists community, although the church has struggled to find a suitable site.

FOLK BELIEFS

Some indigenous customs and traits have survived in the otherwise Catholic and Protestant communities. Although the power of folk beliefs has declined over the centuries, many Hondurans believe that certain people have the power to do good or evil based on magic and psychic or supernatural forces. In remote areas people consult priests for advice on marriage, feuds with neighbors, and times of bad luck, much like their ancestors consulted the medicine man.

FOLK MEDICINE

Many Hondurans have very limited access to modern Western medicine, especially in rural areas. Therefore, folk medicine plays an important role, especially for the poor and those who live in remote regions. Towns usually have a spiritual person who is known for handling illnesses, reminiscent of a traditional medicine man, who is called upon to prescribe herbs and say prayers. Sometimes this person is a midwife, and occasionally it is the storekeeper who sells traditional cures.

Massage and purging are common practices to rid a person of his or her sickness. Many Hondurans also believe foods belong to the "hot" or "cold" category and that one or the other should be avoided or prescribed to cure common ailments. "Hot" foods such as coffee, oranges, and beef are believed to irritate the digestive system. "Cold" foods such as coconuts, bananas, salt, and most kinds of seafood are believed to cause stomach upset. Herbs are also divided into hot or cold and are used to treat illnesses.

A Mayan Catholic altar in a Chorti Indian's home.

Many indigenous groups have their own religions that exist alongside Christianity and include elements of African and Indian animism and ancestor worship.

LANGUAGE

A young Lenca girl holds a Spanish sign that reads "Lenca children want better education and medical attention" during a protest in Honduras.

T HE OFFICIAL LANGUAGE of Honduras is Spanish. English, however, is the main language of the Bay Islands. English is also spoken to some extent in the large cities. A few indigenous languages are still spoken today in remote regions.

SPANISH

Just as the colonial Spanish explorers brought their customs, they also brought their language. However, like most Latin American countries, Hondurans do not speak Castilian Spanish, the official standard Spanish of Spain that originated in the Castile region.

All Spanish gender-specific forms of nouns and adjectives—masculine nouns generally end in "o" and feminine nouns end in "a," and the adjectives used to describe the nouns agree with their gender. For example, "the little boy" is *el chiquito muchacho* (el chee-KEE-toh moo-CHAH-choh). "The little girl" is *la chiquita muchacha* (lah chee-KEE-tah moo-CHAH-chah).

All official and most local signs are in Spanish, the national language of Honduras.

It is estimated that fewer than one thousand people speak the Pech language today.

Spanish also has formal and informal forms of words. The familiar form of "you" is *tú*, and the more formal form is *vos*. In daily conversations between Hondurans who know one another well, the familiar *tú* is used.

Hondurans, like other Latin Americans, often use diminutives to soften what they are saying, making speech more familiar, affectionate, and compassionate. For instance, instead of saying *momento* (moh-MAIN-toh), which means "a moment," they will say *momentito* (moh-main-TEE-toh), which makes "Just a minute!" sound a little more apologetic.

OTHER LANGUAGES

English is the main language spoken in the Bay Islands. Black and white immigrants from the Antilles, the main group of islands in the West Indies, and from Belize (formerly called British Honduras) settled in the Bay Islands near the end of the colonial period and have kept their island version of English alive. Arabic is also spoken on the Bay Islands by immigrants from the Middle East.

Traditional native languages are mostly isolated within remote indigenous communities. However, there are various slang words in the Spanish-speaking Ladino culture that are Indian in origin. There are also many names of places, towns, and streets that are derived from Nahuatl, the language of the Mexican allies of the Spanish conquerors. The Pipil people (related to the Chortí Indians) near the El Salvadoran border still speak a language related to Nahuatl. The large indigenous group, the Lencas, speak various dialects

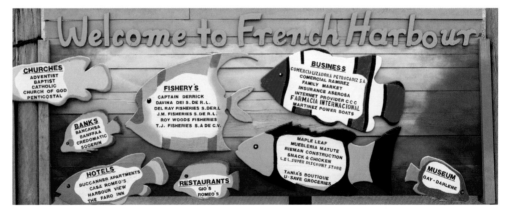

An English language signboard. English is another popular language in Honduras.

HONDURAS'S UNWRITTEN LANGUAGES

Some indigenous languages in Honduras do not have a written alphabet or text. The Pech of northeastern Honduras is an example. In an attempt to keep the Pech language alive in the midst of the predominantly Spanish Honduran culture, some linguists have been working in recent years to develop a written language. First these linguists, together with Pech teachers, had to create an alphabet.

The Pech has a very complicated vowel system—long vowels, short vowels, nasal vowels, glottal vowels, and vowels with an aspiration after them. But most complicated of all, Pech has high and low tones that are very difficult to represent in writing. Many people have collaborated on this project and the first two books in Pech were printed in 1996 using the new alphabet. A Spanish-Pech dictionary and books for second graders are also being prepared for publication. Although the Ministry of Education has not set an official schedule to launch the Pech language program in schools, it will soon be taught in every Pech school. The Pech have expressed their gratitude for the effort to preserve their language by naming one of their schools after a Honduran linguist who worked on the project.

of their language, although Spanish is being adopted by their communities today. The Miskito Indians continue to speak a language similar to the Miskito of South America.

NONVERBAL COMMUNICATION

Hondurans use their hands and arms a great deal when they speak, especially when they are passionate about a subject. In general, they gesticulate more than Americans do.

In the city, when people greet one another, it is expected that women kiss women, men kiss women, and women kiss men.

COMMON EXPRESSIONS

Terms of endearment are most important in Honduras because the people are very friendly, warm, and caring. Adults speaking to children will often use

Lengua de Señas Hondureñas (LESHO) is a sign language developed for the deaf in Honduras.

Young boys enjoying a conversation. Hondurans of different ethnic backgrounds have a common language base in Spanish.

the term *niño* (NEE-nyo) or *niña* (NEE-nya), which means "child." When Hondurans want to use a term of endearment for a beloved sister or female cousin or friend, they use the term *tita* (TEE-tah). When speaking to a brother or male cousin or friend, they use the term *tito* (TEE-toh). When children want to use a term of endearment for either their mother or grandmother, they say *mamita* (mah-MEE-tah). And when speaking to their father or grandfather, they say *papito* (pa-PIH-toh). Otherwise children refer to parents as "mom" and "pa," or *mamá* (mah-MAH) and *papá* (pah-PAH). But they are careful not to put the accent in the wrong place for *papá*, because "PAH-pah" means "potato" or "Pope"!

Chickens and roosters have come to play a large role in Honduran folktales and expressions. They use the term *henpecked* in an unusual context—from a joke about a Honduran president's parrot that was pecked free of its feathers by chickens in a henhouse. They also use the expression "*Este es mi gallo*" (EHS-teh ehs mee GAH-yo), which means "This is my rooster." This expression was originally used by Hondurans who would bet on a winning rooster during a cockfight, but today it is used to mean something along the lines of "This is mine and it is the best!"

CORRECT COMMUNICATION

IN BUSINESS Business letters in Honduras often begin with an elaborate, fervent, positive greeting, even if the rest of the letter is terribly negative. For example, a common opening sentence would be: "I hope that this letter finds you in the best of health and that all of your family and loved ones are healthy and prospering." A short, brisk letter would appear rude and altogether unkind to a Honduran.

AT A MEETING Hondurans are more verbal than many cultures. Instead of quietly slinking late into a meeting that has started, the latecomer must call out a greeting. Hondurans forgive lateness, but not a person who forgets to say *"Buenos dias!"* (BWAY-nos DEE-as). They exchange this in greeting when they meet and say *"Buenos noches"* (BWAY-nos NAW-chez) when they part. To pass one another without a greeting would be considered very rude.

Schoolgirls doing their Spanish homework.

BEFORE A MEAL When sitting down with someone who is eating, whether he or she is a relative or a business acquaintance, well-mannered Hondurans sit down and say *"Buen provecho"* (boo-en pro-VEH-cho), which means "Much good may it do you!"

SPOKEN AND WRITTEN LANGUAGE

Spanish uses the Roman alphabet, like English. There are, however, a few differences. In Spanish *ch*, *ll*, and *rr* are considered to be single, separate letters. When speaking, *rr* is rolled stronger and longer than a single *r*. The double l (*ll*), on the other hand, sounds more like a y. The letter ñ is also a separate letter. B and v have the same sound. K and w do not exist in the Spanish language, but these letters are found in foreign words that have been adopted by Hondurans.

NAMES AND TITLES

Popular first names in Honduras today for girls are Suyapa (named after the Virgin of Suyapa), Ana, Janice, and Maria. Popular names for boys include Mario, Carlos, José, and Antonio.

When greeting one another, women often embrace and sometimes give each other one kiss on the cheek. Men shake hands, but do not usually embrace. Men do hug children when they are young. Women often hug their own children, even when they are grown up, and will hug other children, too. In the cities, a man may sometimes embrace a woman who is not related to him and kiss her on the cheek. However, in rural areas—where people are more socially conservative—a man would never kiss a woman who is not his wife. Such an action is considered taboo.

Hondurans follow the Spanish custom of forming a double surname by taking the family surname of each parent. For instance, a young woman by the name of Teresa Vásquez González has two surnames—González from her mother and Vásquez from her father. Formally she is known as Señorita Vásquez. If she marries a man by the name of Rodrígez Velez Carboñera, she takes her father's surname, losing her own mother's—Teresa Vásquez de Carboñera or Señora de Carboñera.

For men, after the first mention of their full name, they are called by their father's surname—for instance, Oscar Calderón Hernández is referred to as Señor Oscar Calderón. However, some men prefer to use both surnames.

TITLES Titles are also important in Honduras. Becoming a teacher, lawyer, professor, engineer, architect, or doctor takes a lot of work and determination. Therefore, Hondurans believe that a professional person has earned his or her title and should be spoken of with it. Just as Americans say Doctor Jones, Hondurans say Doctor Moreno, as well as Teacher Avila, Professor Martinez, and Attorney Nuñez.

Respect for elders is extremely important for Hondurans. A male adult is Señor and a female adult who is married is Señora. Someone who is a very well-respected member of a community earns the higher title of Don for a man, and Doña for a woman. If these terms were not used, a person would be very insulted. There is a difference between the big cities and the small villages. In cities it is common to always use the terms Señor or Señora. In the villages Don and Doña are the most acceptable titles when speaking with respect.

NEWSPAPERS AND JOURNALISM

As a poor country with low rate of literacy Honduras has few local newspapers compared to many countries. Popular local newspapers in Spanish include Diario Tiempo, El Haraldo, *and* La Prensa, *while English language newspapers include* Honduras This Week. *Many of the newspapers are linked to local political and business interests. The government regulates journalists closely, requiring all reporters to be registered in the College of Journalists, and that all news editors be Honduran by birth. Journalists in Honduras tend to practice self-censorship when reporting on any topics about which the government or wealthy elite might be sensitive. Reporters have been prosecuted for publishing articles deemed anti-government in the past, and journalists have been vulnerable to violence by powerful nongovernment groups, says a study by Reporters Without Borders in 2007.*

Female journalist Dina Meza won the Amnesty International Special Award for Human Rights Journalism Under Threat in 2007. Meza and her online magazine Revistazo *investigate corruption and abuses by the wealthy and powerful. Most recently, her magazine was in conflict with the private security companies that provide security for many local businessmen and landowners. Some of these security firms operate quite independently of the law and have been accused of harassing and exploiting the workers of their employers.*

ARTS

Colorful baskets woven by local Hondurans.

CHAPTER 10

HONDURAS HAS A RICH combination of Ladino and indigenous traditions. Dance, painting, poetry, and folk crafts draw from traditional Honduran beliefs and folklore as well as modern influences. The promotion of fine arts has been intensified recently thanks to public and private institutions that organize exhibitions and contests where new and old generations of artists can come together.

PERFORMING ARTS

DANCE Dancing is a vital part of Honduran culture. Each department has its own traditional dance. Boys and girls learn this and perform it at festivals. Almost every girl has a traditional dress, always bright and colorful, to be worn on these occasions. Women's skirts are full and the blouses have ruffled collars and sleeves. Men wear full pants and ruffled shirts as well. Many official folk dance groups exist in the cities, whose members are older students. Competitions are intense and attract a large audience. Groups from universities are considered professional. Young girls look up to these university dancers and aspire to be as talented when they are older.

A fire artist performing at an evening event in Honduras.

The drums beat loudly as Hondurans gather around, and the dancers begin to clap and stomp their feet. Faces are illuminated by firelight. Wide smiles and bright eyes reflect enthusiasm. A young dancer darts out into the middle of the circle formed by the crowd and begins to dance with swinging hips and small steps toward the drummers. A moment passes, then a young man joins her in the circle. He dances before her while the audience sends out cheers of encouragement. This is punta.

There are hundreds of well-known traditional dances in Honduras. The *maladio wanaragua* (mah-LAH-dee-oh wah-nah-RAH-gwah) is a mask dance that represents the fight of the Garifunas against England. The *sique* (seek) dance has its origins in the dances of the early Indians. Another popular dance on the north coast is the *mascaro* (mas-KAH-roh), which shows strong African influences. Hondurans also love common Latin American dances such as the samba and salsa.

The Garifunas (Black Carib) of the northern coast have a very important dance that originated on the island of Saint Vincent in the Caribbean. The

Traditional Honduran dancers are a sight to behold in their flouncy skirts.

> ## MARIMBA
>
> *The marimba consists of tuned wooden keys, like a xylophone, attached to resonators that hang below the keys to amplify the sound. Common resonators are gourds or wooden bell shapes. The marimba produces sound when its keys are struck with a rubber-tipped stick.*
>
> *There are three kinds of marimba. The simplest is the marimba con tecomates (MAH-reem-bah kon te-koh-MAH-tez), which is worn by one person over the shoulders and held with straps to place the instrument horizontally across the waist. It is associated with rural ceremonial events.*
>
> *The marimba doble (DOH-bley) is really two instruments played as one by seven men. It is set up on the ground with removable legs. It is associated with urban centers and commercial, professional activities, and is found at large festivals.*
>
> *The marimba sencilla (sen-SI-lah) is a single instrument played by three men. It also stands on the ground. Because it is smaller than the doble and bigger than the con tecomates, the sencilla is played at a wide range of events, in rural and urban areas.*

punta (POOHN-tah) is traditionally danced when a relative dies so that the spirit stays on Earth. It is also said to be a dance invoking fertility. However, the influence of the *punta* has stretched far beyond traditional boundaries. Young girls learn the dance from older sisters. Teenagers and young adults do the punta in discos around the country. And people come from all around the world to watch the original *punta* dancers, the Garifunas, in the city of La Ceiba.

MUSIC It is common to hear the music of a marimba band in full swing at any hour of the day or night. Like all Latin Americans, Hondurans love music. They love boleros or anything with a cha-cha rhythm and a lively beat. Honduran music has developed into varied rhythms and styles recalling the religious and folkloric traits of each ethnic group. There are few professional musical groups aside from marimba bands. There are a few classical music groups and a symphony orchestra, too. Two large annual music festivals bring both symphony and folk composers and performers together to celebrate music. Based in La Ceiba, Guillermo Anderson is Honduras's best-known musician, combining *punta*, rock, and salsa for a very Honduran sound. Some consider his song "*En Mi Pais*" an alternative national anthem in Honduras.

The marimba is the best-loved and most representative instrument of Central America. It was introduced to Honduras by African slaves, but its origin can be traced from Southeast Asia, through Africa, to Latin America. Modern adaptations and improvements of the instrument are attributed to Central America. A *marimbero* (mah-rim-BAY-roh) is a person who plays the marimba. There are various forms of the marimba, but usually a whole ensemble, not just one person, plays a large, multifaceted one. Members of a marimba ensemble are usually men from the same family. There are a few women ensembles today, but a mixed gender group would be quite unusual. Children's groups in schools are either a boys' group or a girls'.

Other popular musical instruments are the *caramba* (cah-RAHM-bah), a string instrument found mostly in rural areas, and acoustic and classical guitars.

OTHER PERFORMING ARTS Honduras does not have a major theater tradition. There are small drama groups, and towns and villages have their own small groups that dramatize religious stories during festivals.

Traditional puppet shows are performed in some towns and cities and are enjoyed by both children and adults.

ARCHITECTURE

The ornate temples and elaborately constructed buildings and pyramids of the ancient Maya influence how modern Hondurans build and decorate their buildings. Tegucigalpa's Concordia Park is dedicated to the memory of the Maya with a miniature Mayan temple that shows their distinctive and elaborate ornamentation. In the larger cities of Honduras, intricate carvings and designs of the pre-Columbian era have been artfully integrated into Spanish colonial architecture.

A central plaza, or square, forms the heart of most towns. Important government buildings face it, as does a Catholic chapel or cathedral. The colonial influence—large, arched doorways and domes atop churches—is seen in many buildings in the plazas. These old-style buildings stand in stark

Valázquez is probably the most celebrated Honduran painter. He is internationally known for his primitivist paintings of his village of San Antonio de Oriente, a 16th-century mining center high in the mountains southeast of Tegucigalpa. Valázquez was a barber by profession, without any formal artistic training. He began to paint in 1927 and moved to San Antonio de Oriente in 1930, where he was the town barber and telegraph operator. His unique primitive paintings reflect the humble tranquility of that village where he spent most of the next 30 years of his life.

Valázquez and his paintings were not discovered until 1943 when he met Dr. Wilson Popenoe, director of the Agricultural School at El Zamorano. Popenoe hired him as a barber at the school but encouraged him to market his paintings in Tegucigalpa where they sold for low prices. In 1954 Popenoe organized an exhibition of Valázquez's paintings in Washington, D.C., where the artist gained international acclaim. In 1955 he was given the National Prize for Art, Honduras's most important award for art. He was also elected mayor of San Antonio de Oriente. Valázquez's son and grandson have carried on his primitivist traditions. Valázquez's work is on permanent display in many of Tegucigalpa's finest hotels and galleries.

contrast to the skyscrapers in Tegucigalpa and San Pedro Sula, which use the latest building materials, technology, and design. They house mostly government offices and big, often foreign, businesses. In front of these modern buildings there are still the quaint shaded cantinas where many Hondurans feel most comfortable.

VISUAL ARTS

PAINTING makes up the strongest base in the modern artistic development of Honduras. Most people believe that the fine arts in Honduras were founded by José Miguel Gomez in the 18th century with his religious paintings. Although they show a European influence, they have a distinctly Honduran style. Contemporary Honduran painting began in the 1920s. Today self-taught painters all over the country are dedicated to depicting beautiful, primitive Honduran landscapes and modest towns.

One of the best-known painters in Honduras is Arturo López Rodezno (1908—75). To train new artists he founded the National School of Arts and Crafts. His paintings and school have influenced artists in Honduras and all over the world. José Antonio Valázquez is famous for his paintings depicting life in his village, San Antonio de Oriente, which give the world a window into Honduran life. His most famous painting is of Tegucigalpa's main square with the statue of Francisco Morazán.

A favorite painter in Honduras is Dilber Padilla, who is known for his use of vibrant colors, especially red. His work is considered enigmatic, suggestive, impressionistic, and contemporary. He claims inspiration from Van Gogh and a contemporary Guatemalan artist, Elmar Rojas. Cruz Bermudez is a Garifuna painter who loves natural settings and paints endangered species to publicize environmental issues.

A popular theme in painting is the "Rain of Fish," showing hundreds of fish raining down from the sky. It is based on a Honduran phenomenon where villagers in the department of Yoro woke up after a June thunderstorm to find the ground strewn with fish! One explanation of the strange event is that these fish followed a low-pressure system in from the sea near the end of their lifespan. They leapt ashore during the storm and suffocated. It is not hard to imagine why this fantastic event has inspired so many painters over the years.

LITERATURE

Authors in Honduras traditionally started their careers as newspaper journalists because there were not many local magazines. Honduran newspapers typically print poems, essays, and short stories, so budding writers can publish and polish their work in the papers and at the same time develop a readership. An author who has a following would then approach a publisher with a collection of poems, essays, or short stories, or a novel and may pay to have the work published. Because of the cost involved in becoming a published writer, authors in Honduras are often wealthy and not representative of the common Honduran.

There are few young adult and children's books written in Honduras, as such literature is not very profitable yet. Children's books come from Spain,

In recent years Honduran art objects and folk crafts have been exported for sale in the developed world, especially North America. This business earns valuable foreign currency for the country.

José Trinidad Reyes (1797–1855)

Reyes, known as the Father of Higher Education in Honduras, was multitalented—a playwright, poet, politician, and educator. He was born in Tegucigalpa to poor parents, and his humble origins prevented him from furthering his studies in Comayagüela. He went to Nicaragua, where he graduated with a degree in philosophy, theology, and canon law. In 1822 he was ordained a Catholic priest. In 1840 he was named bishop of Honduras by Rome, but political intrigue prevented him from assuming this position. Reyes was opposed to the president of Honduras, Zelaya y Ayes, so Ayes told Rome that Reyes had died! Under a new president, Reyes turned a literary academy into the first university in Honduras, Universidad Nacional Autonóma de Honduras. He was named its first rector. In 1846 Reyes was named poet laureate of Honduras. He is known for bringing the first printing press and the first piano to Honduras and Tegucigalpa, respectively. Reyes's book on physics was a textbook in Honduras for many years.

Lucila Gamero de Medina (1873–1964)

Medina wrote the first Honduran novel to be published. She was an amazing woman for her time—a physician, an essayist, a feminist, and a novelist. She published many novels during her long and productive life. Her first two novels, Amalia Montiel *and* Adriana y Margarita, *were published in Tegucigalpa in 1893 when she was only 20 years old. They are still read today. Her most famous novel is* Blanca Olmedo *(1903), a controversial attack on the Catholic clergy. Medina was an intelligent, talented, and ambitious woman whom Honduran women admire and try to emulate.*

Mexico, Argentina, and the United States. Most stories are Spanish versions of well-known tales such as "The Tortoise and the Hare."

Several Hondurans have made important contributions to literature. José Cecilio del Valle, the political leader who framed the nation's declaration of independence in the colonial period, was a prominent scholar and newspaper publisher. Poet-historian Rafael Heliodoro Valle, who died in 1959, is also well known. Among writers recognized outside Honduras are José Trinidad Reyes and Ramón Rosa from the earlier years and Juan Molina, Marcos Reyes, and Rafael H. Valle in modern times.

Ramón Amaya Amador (1916—66) is probably Honduras's best-known writer internationally. He began his working life in a banana plantation and went on to become one of the country's most accomplished political journalists and writers. To avoid persecution for his political views he fled first to Guatemala and then to Argentina, returning to Honduras briefly in 1957. He then moved to Prague, Czechoslovakia, to work for a socialist magazine, where he later died in a car crash. None of his works was published in Honduras until the 1990s. His works include *Prisión Verde* (1945), *Biografía de un machete* (1959), *Cipotes* (1963), and *Operación Gorila* (1965).

FOLK ARTS AND CRAFTS

Remnants of pre-Columbian Mayan crafts can be found in Honduras. More common are the contemporary folk crafts sold in markets scattered around Honduras. Many Hondurans are skilled in folk crafts and can usually earn some extra money for their families by selling their products. The wealthy as well as the poor make these traditional crafts as presents for birthdays, baptisms, weddings, and Christmas. Certain areas are renowned for a particular craft such as superb woodcarvings or fine jewelry.

Intricately designed Lenca pottery.

Common Honduran crafts include small wooden or clay hollow animals such as chickens, pigs, dogs, macaws, and other birds. These are painted in many bright colors with intricate designs. A version of this craft has a coin slot in the side to make it into a coin-bank. In order to get the coins out, children have to smash the animal.

Vases are also popular. Black vases of different sizes are painted with tiny, intricate flowers and then filled with large, bright, tropical flowers. Other crafts seen in the markets are handwoven grass bread baskets and laundry baskets. The Garifunas weave a special sleeping mat from a long, slender grass called *nea* (NEH-ah).

GUAMILITO

Guamilito Market in downtown San Pedro Sula is one of the wonderful large city markets of Honduras. It is an excellent place to buy and sell handicrafts from all over Honduras. The most popular items are handwoven hats, large wicker baskets, woodcarvings, miniature paintings, leather goods such as belts, clothing, shoes, and bags, and colorful cotton hammocks. Hand-painted feathers and seeds with minute landscapes are delicate and detailed, as are the intricately carved relief landscapes on cedar. Most artists come to the market themselves to sell their crafts and often bring their whole family. The market is awash with bright tropical colors of crafts, flowers, and fruit.

Over the span of many generations, woodcarving has been honed to a fine art, especially in the town of Valle de Angeles near Tegucigalpa, which is dedicated to crafts. Furniture is one of their specialties. Furniture carved in Valle de Angeles is characterized by its intricate, deep-relief carvings of the village's streets, flowers, and marine life. These craftsmen make coffee tables, mirror frames, and trunks of all shapes and sizes. The wood they use is from the beautiful native cedar tree. Trunks are especially popular. Each takes about a week to make.

Conch shells and colorful mosaics decorate these steps to a house in Honduras.

LEISURE

Soccer is *the* sport in Honduras, especially for these local boys.

U NLESS THEY ARE WEALTHY, Hondurans do not have a lot of time or money for leisure activities. The leisure activities in which they do participate, such as soccer, dancing, and singing, are highly valued. Most Hondurans spend their leisure time with their families.

SPORTS

Young boys play the most sports. At school there is time at recess to be physically active with other boys. Sometimes on Sundays time will be taken for a game or two.

SOCCER is by far the most popular sport for boys and men to play, as well as to watch. Association football, as soccer is called in Honduras, is the national sport, and run by the Federación Nacional Autónoma de Fútbol de Honduras (FENAFUTH). In order to become a hero, one need only be an outstanding soccer player. Honduran boys can enjoy a fast game of soccer, while claiming it is too hot to work in the fields. Hondurans passionately follow the sport at the local, national, and international levels. Emotions often run high. Hondurans listen to big games on the radio, as many people do not have television. Almost every town has a soccer team.

Children having fun on a hammock at a beach in Honduras.

Internet use has become increasingly popular in Honduras, but today only a tiny minority of wealthy people and businesses have access to the Internet. Internet cafés exist in the cities and most major towns and villages.

113

OTHER SPORTS Basketball is quickly becoming popular in the cities of Honduras. Private schools have teams for basketball, volleyball, tennis, and baseball. Golf is played near the bigger cities by wealthy men. Sports for women have not been very popular in Honduras.

Sport fishing is also popular among the wealthy. Along the Caribbean coast and on the Bay Islands people come from all over to fish for tuna, barracuda, shark, blue and white marlin, sailfish, wahoo, mahi-mahi, grouper, kingfish, and red snapper.

People also come from all over the world to dive and snorkel at the coral reefs of the Bay Islands. The water is warm and clear and underwater visibility is very good. It is mostly the wealthier Hondurans who take part in these activities.

LEISURE ACTIVITIES

Dance and song have long been very important to Hondurans. Young girls usually learn the traditional dance of their department, as well as the popular punta dance at a young age. Many city girls go on to take ballet or

Local men fishing at a dock in La Ceiba.

other forms of dance classes. In the absence of sports activities for the majority of girls, dancing gives girls the physical activity and "team" fun they need.

There are many songs about Honduras that boys and girls alike learn when they are very young. The national anthem is popular, and both Honduran children and adults feel proud when they sing it. Girls will often sing and dance during recess and after school if they have any free time.

University students enjoying a chess game in between classes.

While the boys are playing soccer, young girls play outdoors with their friends and cousins. They enjoy a game called *landa* (LAHN-dah) where a group of children stand in a circle and push each other around, catching one another when they fall. Older girls spend the evening with friends. On weekends dancing at the local disco is the most popular activity. Even small towns have discos where teenagers dance the *punta* and other popular Latin American dances, and also dance to popular music from the United States.

People also enjoy going to the beach, especially during national holidays. Hondurans swim, sunbathe, picnic, and surf whenever they can. Other activities that may challenge the mind and pass away the hours include cards, chess, and checkers. But most often in the evenings, Hondurans simply spend time with their families discussing the day's events.

As in most large cities of the world, people who have the time, interest, and a little extra money take classes in almost anything. Tegucigalpa offers classes in acting, guitar, drawing, painting, chess, and many forms of dance. Tegucigalpa even has a cigar club.

The radio is still a popular source of entertainment in rural areas because few homes have television. Television is more popular in the cities, with more than 90 percent of homes in Tegucigalpa estimated to have television. Television programs are in Spanish and include Western movies, cartoons, and game shows from the United States translated into Spanish and programs from Mexico, including many popular soap operas.

STORYTELLING

Storytelling is a popular activity among Honduran families, with grandparents and other elders passing their evenings telling children folktales. Dramatic storytelling is an event during festivals that the celebrants thoroughly enjoy. Stories include tales about the Spanish colonials, animals like horses and chickens, spirits, and thieves. Some stories are intended to teach moral lessons. Others are told in the form of jokes.

One of the most popular characters in Honduran oral literature is the duende, a short man who lives in the woods. Some of the stories about duende are told by parents to frighten children so that they will not stray into the woods. The most famous theme for duende stories is his attempt to get young girls to fall in love with him.

ROOSTERS IN HONDURAN CULTURE

Chickens show up all over Honduran culture. Chickens are kept not just for eggs and meat, but also as pets.

A very popular leisure activity is cockfighting. In the Ladino

Two aggressive roosters battle in a cockfight in Honduras.

culture cockfighting is an acceptable form of sport, and cockfights are considered an essential part of many patron saint festivals. Men who own fighting roosters carry them to distant villages for cockfighting events.

Duende Story

Duende stories are popular with young girls. This is a favorite in many Ladino villages:

Years ago in a little village, there was a group of beautiful young women. As the day of Saint Anthony, the patron saint of the area, came near, these women decided to go into the woods in search of firewood for the upcoming celebrations. On their way they talked happily about the fair. After collecting wood, each gathered up her bundle and began to haul it back to the village.

Suddenly the youngest woman, who was trailing at the back of the group, saw a beautiful flower. She put down her bundle to pick the flower. As soon as she picked it, another one bloomed a few steps away. Each time she picked one, an even prettier one appeared up ahead. She kept collecting flowers until she realized she was lost. She could only see a wonderful world of flowers and hear a faint whistling. As she saw the most beautiful flower yet, she thought of her patron saint and exclaimed, "This is the most beautiful flower I have seen in my entire life. I will cut it and put it on the altar of blessed Saint Anthony." As soon as she said these words, all the flowers disappeared. At that instant her companions, who had been looking for her, found her, and she told them what had happened.

Since that day, every time the festival of Saint Anthony draws near, the people of the village hear melodic whistles from an unseen person and smell the aroma of sweet flowers. The people say the duende must have wanted to carry the young woman away but failed because she was protected by her patron saint. Every year he comes back again, looking for a beautiful woman to carry away and keep him company.

Chicken Folktale

Hondurans are always on the lookout to protect their chickens from deadly encounters with hawks and cats. This story is about chickens and a hawk:

Among the Garifunas, men and boys fish and women and girls take care of the fields and animals. A mother complained to her son that a hawk was carrying off the family's chickens one by one. She asked him to stay home to help her watch over the chickens. The boy did not want to miss any fishing, but he did want to help his mother. So he tied all of the chickens together by their feet before he left to go fishing, thinking it would keep the hawk from being able to carry them away. Instead, the hawk was able to steal all of the chickens at once rather than one by one.

FESTIVALS

Faithful Catholics celebrate Palm Sunday, the start of
Holy Week, with floats and parades in Tegucigalpa.

HONDURAS HAS MANY NATIONAL holidays, both religious and secular. It is a country that knows how to forget its poverty on occasions and celebrate. For official national holidays, employers are required to pay employees for the days off, even if it is a Sunday.

In 2009, 14 days were listed as public holidays, when businesses would be closed. Most festivals are celebrated as street fairs with singing and traditional dancing. Extended families get together to spend the fiesta together.

CELEBRATING SECULAR HOLIDAYS

Many of the secular festival days are celebrated in a small way in the community. There are many days that honor people or ideas. Language Day is celebrated mostly in school by students participating in competitions. Teachers choose the students with the best vocabulary, spelling, and writing. On Teachers' Day, students bring their teachers flowers, candy, or fruit. Tree Day celebrates the trees that provide our world with oxygen whereas Environment Day honors trees, plants, animals, and water. Labor Day is honored by Hondurans staging peaceful protests in the cities.

A girl dresses as an angel in a procession in honor of Saint Michael the Archangel.

A woman lights a candle honoring the Virgin of Suyapa. Thousands of Catholics from all over Central America go to Honduras each year to honor the patron saint during the Festival of Suyapa.

Many campesinos will take the long bus ride or walk to Tegucigalpa on this day to celebrate the power of laborers in Honduras. The celebration of Independence Day starts early in the morning with many marching bands parading through the cities and towns of the country. Each band wears different colors and includes cheerleaders.

New Year's Eve is a special celebration. Everyone buys or makes new clothes for New Year's Day and wears them to Mass on New Year's Eve. They return home, and at midnight everyone, including any young children who can stay awake, goes outside to wish all their neighbors a happy, prosperous new year. Dancing and music, as always, are a part of the celebration.

BIRTHDAYS

Birthdays in Honduras are often only celebrated for children. Adults recognize their birthdays and may receive presents, but there is usually no fiesta. Children, on the other hand, get the best party their parents can afford. They will receive presents if their parents have the money. Typically, the whole extended family is invited over for a fiesta. A large piñata is made by the birthday child's mother, grandmother, or aunt. This is a papier-mâché animal filled with little presents and candy made from sugarcane that is hung from a tree just above the child's head. The birthday child is blindfolded and given a stick with which he or she tries to hit the piñata and break it open to let out all the goodies, which are shared with everyone.

RELIGIOUS HOLIDAYS

Hondurans celebrate the Roman Catholic calendar of religious holidays. They also celebrate the Day of Suyapa, the Virgin Mary, who is the patron saint of Honduras, on February 3. The Feria de Suyapa (Festival of Suyapa) normally lasts a week, from February 2 to 11, and attracts pilgrims from all over Central America.

CHRISTMAS December 24, Christmas Eve, is the most important day of the Christmas season for Hondurans, but Christmas Day is the national holiday. Some of the Christmas traditions familiar to Christians around the world are also practiced in Honduras. A Christmas tree is put up in the home with the nativity scene next to it. The baby Jesus is covered with a small blanket until Christmas Eve, when he is unveiled, representing the birth of Christ.

Most Hondurans attend Mass on Christmas Eve. After church, people visit relatives until midnight, when everyone goes outside to wish their neighbors a merry Christmas. Then there is a large feast until early morning. Most Hondurans exchange gifts, but these are usually presents made for one another, especially for the children.

THREE KINGS' DAY The Epiphany, on January 6, is the day that celebrates the presentation of Jesus Christ to the Three Kings, or Three Wise Men. Hondurans call the Epiphany Three Kings' Day and celebrate it with their own tradition, by acting out the story of Jesus when he was 12 years old and went to Jerusalem alone. In this Bible story, Joseph and Mary were worried and went looking for Jesus. They found him in the temple speaking with the rabbis. In Honduran villages actors playing the parts of Mary and Joseph go around to homes in the neighborhood knocking on doors and asking if anyone has seen young Jesus. Finally, "Mary" and "Joseph" find Jesus in the village church, where they ask the famous question "Where were you?," to which Jesus answers that he is in his Father's house.

La Feria Isidra is celebrated in La Ceiba at the end of May with a week of festivities. It is also known as the Friendship Carnival because people come from all over the world to take part. Each night there are little carnivals in different neighborhoods of the city. The festivities climax with a big parade on the final day, with floats manned by musicians and dancers from Brazil, New Orleans, Japan, Jamaica, Barbados, and many other places.

Garifuna people dancing during a Christmas celebration in Honduras.

HOLY WEEK is an important religious period leading up to Easter. The week starts with Palm Sunday. In Honduras the celebrants act out another Bible story. An actor chosen to act the part of Jesus rides a donkey into town to the church. People lay down palm fronds in front of the donkey to soften the path. Monday, Tuesday, and Wednesday of Holy Week are celebrated by praying in church at the Stations of the Cross—places set up for worshipers to think about Jesus and his suffering. On Holy Thursday Hondurans once again re-create a story from the Bible, usually in a park. Thirteen people act out the Last Supper of Jesus and the 12 apostles.

Cadets from the police academy parade during the Independence Day celebrations in Honduras.

Hondurans eat a special fish soup on Holy Thursday and Good Friday—no meat is eaten. On Good Friday, Hondurans visit the Stations of the Cross once again, but this time each station is acted out by people. At night, the actors become immobile to honor the time when Jesus was entombed. Seven children act as angels to accompany Jesus to heaven.

EASTER is celebrated on Sunday with an elaborate Mass and a family feast afterward. Although there are many Western traditions in Honduras, Hondurans do not have an Easter bunny who brings chocolate and Easter eggs.

CITY AND VILLAGE FESTIVALS

Every city and village has at least one annual festival to celebrate the patron saint of the town or district. People gather from all over the department—and sometimes even the country—to take part, depending on the size of the festival. Local dance groups perform the region's traditional dance as well as the ever-popular *punta*. Marimba music fills the air and people sing along to traditional songs.

Sometimes these annual festivals are secular—the Orange Festival in the department of El Paraíso in southern Honduras is an example. Often annual

January 1	New Year's Day
April 14	Day of the Americas
April 23	Language Day
May 1	Labor Day
Second Sunday in May	Mother's Day
May 30	Tree Day
June 5	Environment Day
June 9	José Trinidad Cabañas Day
June 12	Students' Day
June 14	Flag Day
July 14	Democracy Day
July 20	Lempira Day
August 3	Ethnic Day
September 10	Children's Day
September 15	Independence Day
September 17	Teachers' Day
September 28	Declaration of Independence
October 2	Discovery of Honduras
October 3	Francisco Morazán's Birthday/Soldiers's Day
October 12	Columbus Day and Dia de la Raza
October 21	Armed Forces' Day
October 24	National Union's Day
November 18	Nationality Day
November 22	José Cecilio de Valle Day

festivals are religious in nature, usually celebrating the patron saint of the place. At the village of Campa in southwestern Honduras, for example, an annual festival honors the villagers' patron saint, San Matias. People celebrate with traditional Indian dances called the *guancasco* (goo-ahn-CAS-coh) and the *garrobo* (gah-ROH-boh).

FOOD

A local waitress in Copán balances a drink on her head as she shows off the delicious Honduran fare.

MOST HONDURANS EAT the same food day in and day out unless they are wealthy. In the rural areas people usually eat only what they can produce themselves. They cannot afford to buy a variety of foods. But they enjoy food so much that feasts are a part of every fiesta.

Urban people generally are better nourished—because they buy what they need, their diet tends to have a better balance of food groups. However, most Hondurans in the cities do not eat well by American standards. They rarely eat meat, and close to payday they may eat very little.

STAPLES

The typical diet of a Honduran is based on corn. It is the most widely planted crop, cheapest in the marketplace, and grown all year-round. Women turn corn into tortillas every day. Red beans are the main source of protein. Mixing beans together with corn provides a complete protein. When beans are eaten alone, the body misses out on the essential amino acids that mixing corn with beans provides. People in Honduras and other Central American countries have come to understand this, which is why beans and corn tortillas are eaten daily, sometimes at every meal.

White rice is also a staple food. Cassava, another important food, is a tropical plant with a large starchy root. Plantains, which resemble bananas, are used in many recipes.

When eating out, most Hondurans will order a national dish called the *plato típico* (typical dish) because it is filling and inexpensive, besides being a favorite. It includes a combination of beans, rice, tortillas, fried bananas, beef or fish, potatoes or cassava, cream, cheese, and a cabbage or tomato salad. Many restaurants in cities or small towns offer a cheap, large, fast meal to workers at lunchtime called *plato del día*. The meals differ from place to place but always include tortillas.

OTHER TYPICAL FOODS

Most rural families own a cow, and from the milk, the women make *cuajada* (kwah-HAH-dah), a kind of cottage cheese that is slightly different from the North American cottage cheese. Most Hondurans do not drink milk as a beverage but eat the cream, sour cream, and cheese the milk provides. Although almost every rural household raises chickens and pigs, it is a rare treat to have meat. On rare occasions pork is eaten, perhaps as a dish at a feast during a fiesta. Fish is more commonly eaten, especially in coastal towns. Hondurans usually eat their fish fried or in soups and stews.

Fried bananas, a popular snack, are often sold in the marketplace. *Tajaditas* (tah-jah-DEE-tahs), or crispy fried banana chips, and sliced green mangoes sprinkled with salt and cumin are sold in bags on the street.

Green vegetables are often missing from the diet, but peppers, especially hot chili peppers, are eaten with many meals. Hondurans, especially the rural poor, also eat sweet bread. Among the people living on the Caribbean coast, coconut bread is eaten almost daily.

POPULAR DISHES

Nacatamales (nah-kah-tah-MAH-les)—large corn cakes stuffed with vegetables and meat—are usually bought in the marketplace or made by those who can afford meat. *Tapado* (tah-PAH-doh), a dish from the Black Carib, is a stew made with meat or fish, vegetables, and cassava. *Sopa de mondongo* (SOH-pah de moan-DOAN-goh) is a stew made with chopped tripe, part of a cow's stomach.

Baleada (bah-lay-AH-dah) is another daily favorite. This is a warm corn or flour tortilla folded over refried beans, crumbled cheese, and sour cream. Baleadas are often sold cheaply at markets, street stands, or food shacks. Another favorite street food is *tortillas con quesillo*—two crisp, fried corn tortillas with melted white cheese between them. Fried chicken is also a favorite food.

A woman prepares the fire for her sand oven.

Honduran food is tasty and sometimes spicy hot. Hondurans use chili peppers, tomatoes, soy sauce, salt, black pepper, cilantro, cumin, onions, sweet peppers, garlic, and beef or chicken stock cubes as a base for soups.

DRINKS

Honduran adults drink coffee with almost every meal, but do not often drink tea. *Culey* (KOO-lee) is a very sweet fruit juice drunk especially by children. *Guifiti* (gwee-FEE-tee) is a tea-like herbal drink that tickles the taste buds and is drunk to detoxify the body. Sodas and colas are found everywhere today, including a few local flavors like banana. Most Hondurans do not drink unflavored milk but *licuados*, milk blended with fruit, are popular.

It is unusual for Hondurans to drink alcohol with a meal. Alcoholic drinks include *aguardiente* (ah-gwar-dee-EHN-teh), translated as "fire water," a homemade liquor that tastes of licorice, and wine, including *vino de coyol* (VEE-noh de KO-yohl), a sparkling wine made from the sap of the coyol palm. There are also four kinds of beer made and consumed in Honduras.

KITCHENS

Women almost always do the cooking. It is very rare to find a man cooking in the kitchen.

In rural homes kitchens are usually outdoors. A woman has an adobe and sand oven called a *lorena* (loh-REH-nah) for baking breads. These ovens have no door and are approximately waist-high. Women burn firewood in them for two hours to get the oven hot enough to bake bread. The dough sits in small pans that are placed into the oven by hand. After 20 minutes the bread is usually done, and the loaves are removed from the oven with a long wooden paddle.

A rural woman will often have a wood-fire stove going as well to fry food or boil stews. People who can afford it will have this stove indoors in a kitchen. But even in the cities, an indoor kitchen is not used by everyone.

DAILY MEALS

Every meal is generally eaten at home. Children who have many miles to walk to school will eat a meal provided by the school during the day. Some people in the cities go to restaurants for supper on special occasions.

Hondurans often eat fruit when they want something sweet. The type of fruit eaten depends on the region. Those who live on the Caribbean coast have the greatest variety. The most popular are bananas, pineapples, mangoes, papayas, and berries.

> ## PINEAPPLES
>
> *Pineapples have been cultivated in Honduras since pre-Columbian times and have therefore made their way into the Honduran diet. Although pineapples are grown commercially around La Ceiba, many families grow pineapples in their yard or family plot.*
>
> *Every part of the pineapple can be used, even the outside prickly skin, which makes good pineapple tea or vinegar. One of the most popular ways for Hondurans to preserve vegetables is to pickle them in pineapple vinegar. The fruit is pulped for juice to drink and jam for pies. Pineapple tops are put in a bucket with a little water for a month. If roots appear, they go back to the family plot for planting and start all over again.*

A typical lunch, made up of fluffy rice and meat.

Meals are seldom eaten around a table. If there is no table, the family sits on chairs around the room. Some families eat outdoors because the space inside is too small. Those who have a television may sit around and watch it while they eat. Otherwise, they eat and talk about their day. Wealthier people have a separate room for dining.

Meals are eaten with spoons, forks, and knives, and tortillas and breads are eaten held in the hand.

BREAKFAST The morning meal is eaten only after some of the morning chores are done. Breakfast may include a combination of the following: red beans and tortillas, eggs, cheese (often *cuajada*), plantains, salty butter on bread, coffee, and even homemade cereal with milk. Poor Hondurans have coffee with bread for breakfast.

LUNCH is usually more substantial than breakfast and may include meat if the family can afford it. A typical lunch would have white rice with pork, beef, or chicken, a soup made of red beans, fish or chicken, and tortillas. *Culey* is often drunk during lunch.

Candy in Honduras is dulce de rapadura, basically a processed sugar cube made from sugarcane and wrapped in cane leaves or corn husks. Dulce, as it is called, is usually made by only one campesino in a given village. Sugarcane stalks are cut down and put through a sugar mill powered by cows attached to horizontal wooden braces. The cows walk in a circle to turn the press, and juice from the sugarcane is squeezed out.

The juice is collected, cooked, and then cooled in wooden molds. There may be as many as 50 large molds in one very large rectangular piece of wood. The end product is sold to other people in the village or taken to a market elsewhere. Aside from being eaten as candy, dulce is used to sweeten coffee, make fruit preserves, or to sweeten breads.

SUPPER is generally a lighter meal than lunch. It usually includes a soup, red beans, eggs, plantains, butter, and tortillas. Meat is not commonly eaten at this meal, even by those who can afford it. Fried beans with onions eaten with a tortilla is popular.

DESSERT Most Hondurans do not eat dessert because they cannot afford the luxury. Where there is dessert, perhaps at a fiesta, sweet cake and ice cream are favorites. *Dulce de rapadura* (DOOL-say de rah-pah-DUHR-ah), a candy made from sugarcane juice, is the most common Honduran dessert.

Fried tortillas and other Honduran snacks are typical fast foods sold on the streets and in markets.

FEASTS

For fiestas and town festivals, the meals are not very different from everyday meals. But some of the favorites are made for the community party, such as *nacatamales*. Pork, beef, and chicken are commonly reserved for special occasions.

PANQUECAS DE BANANAS (PLANTAIN PANCAKES)

4 servings

3 very ripe plantains

3 tablespoons (45 ml) flour

4 tablespoons (60 ml) melted butter

²/₃ cup (170 ml) cooked beans

²/₃ cup (170 ml) lard

- Boil the plantains then mash them.
- Add the flour and butter, and mix thoroughly.
- Fry the beans for about five minutes in a tablespoon (15 ml) of lard.
- Heat remaining lard in another frying pan; add one tablespoon (15 ml) of the plantain mixture at a time to make a small pancake, spreading with a fork to give shape.
- Fry the pancakes for about five minutes.
- Now place one teaspoon (5 ml) of the fried beans on each pancake, and fold. Fry the stuffed pancakes, covered, three minutes on each side, or until brown.

COCONUT BREAD

8—10 servings

4 ounces (110 g) margarine

6 ounces (170 g) raw cane sugar

10 ounces (280 g) whole meal flour

2 tablespoons (30 ml) baking powder

½ tablespoon (10 ml) ground cinnamon

6 ounces (170 g) freshly grated coconut

½ pint (300 ml) soy milk

- Combine the margarine and raw cane sugar until well blended to form a creamed mixture.

- Sift the flour, baking powder, and ground cinnamon in a separate bowl. Stir in the grated coconut.

- Add the dry ingredients with the soy milk to the creamed mixture, mixing it to a thick dough-like consistency.

- With floured hands so the mixture does not stick, divide the mixture and shape into buns.

- Place the buns on a greased baking sheet, spacing well apart, and bake in a preheated oven at 350°F (180°F) until risen and brown.

A　　　**B**　　　**C**　　　**D**

1

BELIZE

Swan Islands

Roatán Island

Guanaja Island

Bay Islands (Islas de la Bahía)

Gulf of Honduras

Utila Island

Cayos Cochinos Islands

2 GUATEMALA

Puerto Cortés

Tela

San Pedro Sula

La Lima

El Progreso

La Ceiba

Trujillo

Cordillera Nombre de Dios

▲ Mount Bonito

R. Aguán

Aguán Valley

R. Sico

R. Paulaya

R. Plátano

Biosfera del Río Plátano

Cordillera Merendón

R. Ulúa

El Cajón Reservoir

Yoro

La Unión

Copán

Santa Rosa de Copán

Lake Yojoa

3

Mount Celaque

Mount El Pital ▲

(9,350ft /2,849 m)

Gracias

Siguatepeque

Comayagua

Juticalpa

Patuca Mountains

R. Patuca

Intibucá

La Paz

La Esperanza

Marcala

Valle de Ángeles

Santa Lucía

TEGUCIGALPA

Danlí

El Paraíso

Cordillera Entre, Ríos

R. Coco

EL SALVADOR

Nacaome

R. Choluteca

4

Amapala

Choluteca

Gulf of Fonseca

NICARAGUA

PACIFIC OCEAN

MAP OF HONDURAS

E

Caribbean Sea

Cajones
Cays

Mosquito Coast

Caratasca
Lagoon

● Puerto Lempira

● Capital city
● Major town
▲ Mountain peak

Feet	Meters
16,500	5,000
9,900	3,000
6,600	2,000
3,300	1,000
1,650	500
660	200
0	0

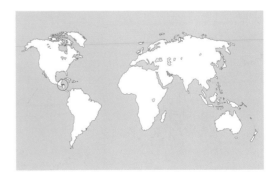

ECONOMIC HONDURAS

OVERVIEW

Honduras is the second-poorest country in Central America. The gap between the rich and the poor is very great, and unemployment has remained high for decades. The economy is dependent on just a few exports, especially bananas and coffee, making it vulnerable to natural disasters and changes in world prices. The United States is Honduras's largest trading partner, and the country relies heavily on the U.S. economy. In 2008 and 2009, Honduras suffered as a result of the recession in the United States. However, the introduction of the U.S.-CAFTA in 2006 has helped increase investment and trade. The country has extensive forest, sea, and mineral resources, although traditional slash-and-burn farming methods continue to destroy Honduran forests.

GROSS DOMESTIC PRODUCT (GDP)

$13.78 billion (2008 estimate)

GDP PER CAPITA

$3,700 (2008 estimate)

CURRENCY

Honduran lempiras (HNL)
$1 = 19.3 HNL (2009 estimate)

LABOR FORCE

2.89 million (2008 estimate)

LABOR FORCE BY TYPE OF JOB

Agriculture: 39.2 percent
Industry: 20.9 percent
Services: 39.8 percent (2005 estimate)

UNEMPLOYMENT RATE

27.8 percent (2007 estimate)

AGRICULTURAL PRODUCTS

Bananas, coffee, citrus, beef, timber, shrimp, tilapia, lobster, corn, African palm

NATURAL RESOURCES

Timber, gold, silver, copper, lead, zinc, iron ore, antimony, coal, fish, hydropower

MAIN INDUSTRIES

Sugar, coffee, textiles, clothing, wood products

MAIN EXPORTS

Coffee, shrimp, bananas, gold, palm oil, fruit, lobster, lumber, to United States (67.2 percent), El Salvador (4.9 percent), Guatemala (3.9 percent) (2007 estimate)

MAIN IMPORTS

Machinery and transportation equipment, industrial raw materials, chemical products, fuels, foodstuffs, from United States (52.4 percent), Guatemala (7.1 percent), El Salvador (5.2 percent), Mexico (4.5 percent), Costa Rica (4.2 percent) (2007 estimate)

CULTURAL HONDURAS

Museo de Antropologia e Historia de San Pedro Sula
This fine museum illustrates the history of the Valle de Sula from pre-Columbian times through the modern era, with hundreds of well-preserved exhibits and artifacts from the region.

La Ceiba
Situated beneath the grand Pico Bonito mountain, this port town is a popular place to holiday, with beaches, restaurants, and entertainment, as well as hosting the annual La Feria Isidra carnival.

Bay Islands
Thirty-one miles (50 km) off the north coast of Honduras, the three islands of Roatan, Utilia, and Guanaja are some spectacular reefs and teem with Caribbean marine life.

Mosquito Coast (Moskitia)
This huge, unique region is home to vast tracts of untamed jungle and is one of Central America's last wilderness frontiers. Every type of animal can be found here, including tapirs, manatees, jaguars, and crocodiles, as well as hundreds of species of birds. Moskitia is also home to indigenous cultures and peoples isolated from civilization.

Biosfera del Rio Platano Nature Reserve
This vast, unspoiled wilderness is one of the most magnificent nature reserves in the region. The extraordinary range of animal life includes endangered species, such as the tapir and giant anteater.

Copán Ruinas
Well-preserved Mayan ruins, sculptures, and hieroglyphs make this one of the great archaeological sites of Central America and now a UNESCO World Heritage site.

Gracias
Originally called *Gracias de Dios* ("Thanks to God"), this small town was the capital of all the Spanish territories in Central America in the 16th century. Today it is home to many colonial-era buildings and cobbled streets.

Lake Yajoa (Lago de Yojoa)
This picturesque lake is a bird spotter's paradise, with more than 400 species of birds making their home here, including the rare quetzal.

Our Lady of Suyapa
In the small town of Suyapa just outside Tegucigalpa is one of Central America's most impressive religious shrines, the Basilica of the Virgin of Suyapa. The Virgin of Suyapa is the patron saint of Honduras and all Central America. The statue is honored inside the massive basilica with magnificent stained glass windows and a marble altar with bronze and gold designs.

OFFICIAL NAME
Republic of Honduras

LAND AREA
43,278 square miles (112,090 sq km)

CAPITAL
Teguciagalpa

ADMINISTRATIVE DEPARTMENTS
18 departments (*departamentos*): Atlantida, Choluteca, Colon, Comayagüela, Copan, Cortes, El Paraiso, Francisco Morazan, Gracias a Dios, Intibuca, Islas de la Bahia, La Paz, Lempira, Ocotepeque, Olancho, Santa Barbara, Valle, Yoro

HIGHEST POINT
Cerro Las Minas: 9,350 feet (2,850 m) above sea level

POPULATION
7,792,854 (2009 estimate)

GENDER RATIO
1.05 male/female (2009 estimate)

AGE STRUCTURE:
0—14 years: 38.1% (male 1,514,544/female 1,451,862)
15—64 years: 58.3% (male 2,278,508/female 2,267,527)
65 years and over: 3.6% (male 125,991/female 154,422) (2009 estimate)

LIFE EXPECTANCY
Total population: 69.4 years
Male: 67.86 years
Female: 71.02 years (2009 estimate)

MEDIAN AGE
20.3 years (2009 estimate)

BIRTHRATE
26.27 births per 1,000 population (2009 estimate)

DEATH RATE
5.41 deaths per 1,000 population (2009 estimate)

ETHNIC GROUPS
Mestizo (mixed Amerindian and European) 90 percent, Amerindian 7 percent, black 2 percent, white 1 percent

RELIGION
Roman Catholic 97%, Protestant 3%

LANGUAGES
Spanish, Amerindian dialects

NATIONAL HOLIDAY
Independence Day, September 15 (1821)

TIME LINE

IN HONDURAS	IN THE WORLD
1502	
Christopher Columbus lands in Honduras.	
1525	
Spain begins its conquest of Honduras, which is achieved in 1539.	
1700s	
The northern coast falls to British buccaneers. A British protectorate is established over the coast until 1860.	**1776** U.S. Declaration of Independence
1821	**1789–99** The French Revolution
Honduras gains independence from Spain but is absorbed into Mexico.	
1840	
Honduras becomes fully independent.	
1932–49	**1939**
Honduras is run by the right-wing National Party of Honduras (PNH) dictatorship, led by General Tiburcio Carias Andino.	World War II begins. **1945** The United States drops atomic bombs on Hiroshima and Nagasaki. World War II ends.
1963	
After a successful coup, Colonel Osvaldo Lopez Arellano takes power.	
1969	
Border disputes leads to a war with El Salvador.	
1974	
Lopez resigns after allegedly accepting a bribe.	
1975	
Colonel Juan Alberto Melgar Castro takes power.	
1978	
Melgar is ousted in a coup led by General Policarpo Paz Garcia.	
1981	
Roberto Suazo Cordova of the centrist Liberal Party of Honduras (PLH) is elected president, leading the first civilian government in more than a century. But army chief General Gustavo Alvarez retains considerable power. U.S. run camps for training Salvadorans in counter-insurgency are set up on Honduran territory.	

IN HONDURAS	IN THE WORLD
1982	
Contras (U.S.-backed Nicaraguan counterrevolutionaries) launch operations.	
1984	
Alvarez is deposed amid anti-American demonstrations in Tegucigalpa. The U.S.-run training camps are shut down.	
1986	
Azcona del Hoyo of the Liberal Party is elected president.	
1989	
General Alvarez is assassinated by left-wing guerrillas in Tegucigalpa.	
1990	
Rafael Callejas sworn in as president; he introduces liberal economic reforms. The last Nicaraguan Contras leave Honduras.	
1993	
Veteran Liberal Party candidate Carlos Reina is elected president. Reina pledges to reform judicial system and limit the power of armed forces.	
1997	**1997**
Carlos Flores of the Liberal Party is elected president; he pledges to restructure the armed forces.	Hong Kong is returned to China.
1998	
Hurricane Mitch devastates Honduras.	
1999	
The armed forces are placed under civilian control.	**2001**
2002	Terrorists crash planes into New York, Washington D.C., and Pennsylvania.
Ricardo Maduro elected president.	**2003**
2005	War in Iraq begins.
Tropical storm Gamma destroys homes. The Liberal Party's Manuel Zelaya is declared the winner of presidential elections.	
2008	
Honduras joins the Bolivarian Alternative for the Americas (ALBA), an alliance that will alleviate the country's chronic poverty.	

GLOSSARY

aguardiente (ah-gwar-dee-EHN-teh)
A local liquor that tastes like licorice.

baleada (bah-lay-AH-dah)
A warm corn or flour tortilla folded over refried beans, crumbled cheese, and sour cream.

campesinos
Male peasants.

cuajada (kwah-HAH-dah)
A Honduran variety of cottage cheese.

culey (KOO-lee)
A very sweet fruit juice.

dulce de rapadura (DOOL-say de rah-pah-DUHR-ah)
Local candy made from sugarcane and wrapped in cane leaves or corn husks.

evangélicos (eh-van-HAY-lee-kohs)
Protestant groups.

guifiti (gwee-FEE-tee)
A tea-like herbal drink.

hacendados (hah-sen-DAH-dohs)
Traditional elite who own land.

Ladino
Spanish-speaking people whose lifestyle follows Hispanic patterns.

landa (LAHN-dah)
A game played by the girls.

lorena (loh-REH-nah)
A sand oven for baking breads.

machismo
Masculine, daring, brave behavior exhibited by men.

manta
White flowing dress material worn by the poor.

marianismo (mah-ree-ahn-EEZ-moh)
Feminine ideal emphasizing self-sacrifice and loyalty to husband and family.

mascaro (mas-KAH-roh)
Popular dance with strong African influence.

mestizo
People who are a racial mix of indigenous (Indian) and European ancestry.

nacatamales (nah-kah-tah-MAH-les)
Corn cakes stuffed with vegetables and meat.

nea (NEH-ah)
A special sleeping mat.

novena
Nine nights of prayer after a family member's death and on the death anniversary.

punta (POOHN-tah)
Traditional dance of the Garifunas, performed after death; today a modern dance in discos.

tajaditas (tah-jah-DEE-tahs)
Crispy fried banana chips.

vino de coyol (VEE-noh de KO-yohl)
A sparkling wine made from the sap of the coyol palm.

FOR FURTHER INFORMATION

BOOKS

Dendinger, Roger E. *Honduras* (Modern World Nations). New York: Chelsea House, 2008.

Foster, Lynn V. *A Brief History of Central America*. New York: Facts on File, 2007.

Gold, Janet N. *Culture and Customs of Honduras* (Culture and Customs of Latin America and the Caribbean). Westport, CT: Greenwood Press, 2009.

Kras, Sara Louise. *Honduras* (Enchantment of the World. Second Series). New York: Children's Press, 2007.

Shields, Charles J. *Honduras* (Central America Today). Broomall, PA: Mason Crest Publishers, 2008.

Zuchora-Walske, Christine. *Honduras in Pictures* (Visual Geography. Second Series). Minneapolis: Twenty-First Century Books, 2009.

FILMS

Dive Travel the Bay Islands Roatán, Utila, and Guanaja. TravelVideoStore.com, 2009.

MUSIC

Music from Honduras. Vols. 1 & 2 (various artists), Caprice, 2001.

Punta Paradise. Vol. 1 (various artists), House of Punta/Stonetree Records, 2006.

Wabaruagun Ensemble. *Honduras: Songs of the Black Caribs*. Ocora France. 2002.

BIBLIOGRAPHY

BOOKS

Ashlie, Malana. *Gringos in Paradise: Our Honduras Odyssey*. Charleston, SC: BookSurge Publishing, 2007.

Chandler, Gary and Liza Prado. *Honduras & the Bay Islands*. Oakland, CA: Lonely Planet, 2007.

Gollin, James D. *Adventures in Nature: Honduras* (Adventures in Nature Series). Emeryville, CA: Avalon Travel Publishing, 2001.

Humphrey, Chris. *Honduras* (Moon Handbooks). Emeryville, CA: Avalon Travel Publishing, 2006.

WEBSITES

Central Intelligence Agency—Honduras, www.cia.gov/library/publications/the-world-factbook/geos/ho.html#Geo

Encyclopedia of the Nations—Honduras, www.nationsencyclopedia.com/economies/Americas/Honduras.html

Honduras, www.honduras.com

Honduras—A Country Study, www.country-data.com/frd/cs/hntoc.html#hn0102

Honduras Hotel Information directory, www.honduras-information.hotelhonduras.com/

Honduras News, http://hondurasnews.com/

Honduras Press, Media, TV, Radio, Newspapers, www.pressreference.com/Gu-Ku/Honduras.html

Honduras This Week, www.hondurasthisweek.com/

Honduras This Week—Environment, www.marrder.com/htw/special/environment/

MongaBay—Honduras, http://rainforests.mongabay.com/20honduras.htm

NationMaster, www.nationmaster.com

Timeline—Honduras, http://news.bbc.co.uk/1/hi/world/americas/country_profiles/1225471.stm

World Information, www.worldinformation.com

The World Bank, http://web.worldbank.org

INDEX

INDEX